BEST OF AUSTRIAN CUISINE

D1110888

Hippocrene is NUMBER ONE in
International Cookbooks

Africa and Oceania
Best of Regional African Cooking
Egyptian Cooking
Good Food from Australia
Traditional South African Cookery
Taste of Eritrea

Asia and Near East
The Best of Taiwanese Cuisine
Imperial Mongolian Cooking
The Joy of Chinese Cooking
Healthy South Indian Cooking
The Indian Spice Kitchen
Best of Goan Cooking
Best of Kashmiri Cooking
Afghan Food & Cookery
The Art of Persian Cooking
The Art of Turkish Cooking
The Art of Uzbek Cooking

Mediterranean
Best of Greek Cuisine
Taste of Malta
A Spanish Family Cookbook
Tastes of North Africa

Western Europe
Art of Dutch Cooking
Best of Austrian Cuisine
A Belgian Cookbook
Cooking in the French Fashion (bilingual)
Celtic Cookbook
Cuisines of Portuguese Encounters
English Royal Cookbook
The Swiss Cookbook
Traditional Recipes from Old England
The Art of Irish Cooking
Feasting Galore Irish-Style
Traditional Food from Scotland
Traditional Food from Wales
The Scottish-Irish Pub and Hearth Cookbook
A Treasury of Italian Cuisine (bilingual)

Scandinavia
Best of Scandinavian Cooking
The Best of Finnish Cooking
The Best of Smorgasbord Cooking
Good Food from Sweden

Central Europe
All Along the Danube
All Along the Rhine
Best of Albanian Cooking
Best of Croatian Cooking
Bavarian Cooking
Traditional Bulgarian Cooking
The Best of Czech Cooking
The Best of Slovak Cooking
The Art of Hungarian Cooking
Hungarian Cookbook
Art of Lithuanian Cooking
Polish Heritage Cookery
The Best of Polish Cooking
Old Warsaw Cookbook
Old Polish Traditions
Treasury of Polish Cuisine (bilingual)
Poland's Gourmet Cuisine
Taste of Romania
Taste of Latvia

Eastern Europe
The Best of Russian Cooking
Traditional Russian Cuisine (bilingual)
The Best of Ukrainian Cuisine

Americas
Argentina Cooks
Cooking the Caribbean Way
Mayan Cooking
The Honey Cookbook
The Art of Brazilian Cookery
The Art of South American Cookery
Old Havana Cookbook (bilingual)

BEST OF
AUSTRIAN CUISINE

Expanded Edition

Written and Illustrated by
Elisabeth Mayer-Browne

HIPPOCRENE BOOKS
New York

Hippocrene expanded paperback edition, 2001.
First Hippocrene paperback edition 1997.
Originally published in 1960 by Wilhelm Frick-Verlag & Co., Vienna.

For information, address:
HIPPOCRENE BOOKS, INC.
171 Madison Avenue
New York, NY 10016

ISBN 0-7818-0884-7

Printed in the United States of America.

Table of Contents

INTRODUCTION

In our age of haste, it is a relief to turn to one of the leisurely arts of bygone days. The speed that propels us through our life is sometimes unavoidable, but often so unnecessary. What becomes of the odd ten minutes you save by driving fast, the hours you saved by taking a plane instead of a train? What you could do with them is to, yes, I dare to say it in this world of Instant food: "Take a little more time for cooking!" Don't think of it as 'household chore' which has to be done, once or twice every day — it used to be thought of as an Art, and it still is! Even everyday life can be made more enchanting by the good and loving preparation of food, and an artist you most certainly are when you have guests who reflect the pleasure of something beautiful to look at, and delicious to taste, which you have yourself created. Sometimes I am really worried, lest in days to come, cooking will be forgotten completely, in common with so many of the other individual arts — how often does one see woodcraft or embroidery being indulged in as part of a home recreation? You may rightly say — "What's the use of worrying?" — unless, ouf course, you're prepared to do something about it! And so, in a way, I feel I am, by writing this book.

Most recipes are common knowledge over here, some are family ones handed down to my mother by her mother and so on. I have simplified these, as my great-grandmother had six maids, my grandmother two, my mother one ... and don't ask about me! But we have tins, frozen food, mixers and other aids galore, which helps discount the human help, so we'll get by. When we think of leisure, the good old days, good living and cooking — which town springs to mind, as having a renowned link with all these things? Why, Vienna of course! Here, life still has the old world charm, here cooking is really still practised as an art, and so many of you have been here and enjoyed it. The other day we met a young American couple on their honeymoon over here, and when asked: "— why did you choose Vienna of all places?" They said: "So many of our friends have been all over Europe. Some liked Paris, some liked it less; some loved Rome most of all, and some didn't, and so on, but the place they all loved was Vienna, and so here we are!"

Well, before you think that this is a travel guide, I shall return to cooking. (But if you haven't been here yet, do come, you'll love it.)

We have a saying here, which I hope I can translate for you: "Liebe geht durch den Magen", which means roughly, Love travels through the stomach, no, that sounds awful, but I suppose you'll know what I mean: Good food is a strong arrow in Cupid's bow, and although your husband may not have married you for your culinary knowledge — it certainly helps! Enough talk for now, let's get down to work, no, to art!

Veal

It is only fair, I think, to start an Austrian cooking book with the most famous of all dishes to have come out of Vienna. So famous, that there is not even a translation for it. You have gueessed right, and here it is:

WIENER SCHNITZEL

Now, please don't say: "No need to tell us how to make a Wiener Schnitzel, we know that all right, everybody does!" I don't want to hurt your feelings, maybe you are really one of the few exceptions. But I am just slightly uneasy, that you might be doing them the way they are done in Germany, with thick brown gravy added, or, as they are served in English restaurants, with some chopped hard boiled eggs and anchovy on top. You don't do it that way? So much the better! Then you are half a Viennese cook already, and all the other recipes will be child's play to you. But let me write down the real way to do a Wiener Schnitzel, just in case!
Trim your Escallopes, make some incisions around the edge and beat them well. Prepare three deep plates; put some flour in one, in the second, beaten egg, with a little cold milk and a pinch of salt, and the third, fill with breadcrumbs. Dip the Escallope first in flour, then shake it so that all the surplus comes off, dip it in the beaten egg, let this also drip off, then finally into the bread-crumbs.

Do everything lightly, softly, lovingly, gently. Do not press down the bread-crumbs, just shake off the surplus. Now into the frying pan. (Escallopes should be fried straight after the flour, egg and bread-crumb coating.) The fat must be smoking, it can be lard or oil, but it should be deep, and there must be plenty of room around each Schnitzel.

Lift out with a pastry slicer, so that the fat can drip off, and serve at once. Delicious with buttered parsley potatoes or rice and salad. Have you tried a dash of cranberry sauce with it? Served separately, not on the Schnitzel. This is something we like in our family, and which is not normally served. But try it anyway, and don't forget a nice wedge of lemon to squeeze on the meat.

The Schnitzel also taste very good when cold, preferably with potato salad.

Veal cutlets can be dealt with in the same way, also Escallopes of pork and pork chops.

PARISIAN ESCALLOPES (Pariser Schnitzel)

Are made the same way, but are dipped into flour and egg only; some people dip into flour, egg and then flour again, if a sligthtly thicker crust is preferred.

ESCALLOPES WITH MUSHROOM FILLING
(Wiener Schnitzel mit Schwammerlfülle)

Trim the Escallopes, but only beat slightly so that they remain thick enough for you to make a small pocket into which you insert the sliced mushrooms. Now dip in flour, egg, bread-crumbs and fry them in the usual way.

ESCALLOPES NATURELLES (Naturschnitzel)

Trim the Escallopes, make incisions, and beat well. Salt and pepper slightly, dip into flour on one side, and put into hot fat (preferably butter) with the floured side first. Fry golden brown on both sides, remove to plate, and keep hot. Pour off surplus fat of frying pan (or spoon it off carefully), add water to the brown "chips" left in the pan, and bring to the boil. Add a knob of butter and pour over Escallope. Serve with any vegetable, potatoes or rice and (or) salad. Some people like stewed apples with it.

ESCALLOPES WITH PAPRIKA (Paprikaschnitzel)

4 Escallopes
¼ pint sour cream = ½ cup
¼ pint water = ½ cup
1 teaspoonful tomato purée (optional)

1 teaspoonful butter
1 teaspoonful flour
salt and pepper

Begin the same way as above. When the meat is fried golden brown, cover with water and add a spoonful of paprika. Simmer for a few minutes, then add a quarter pint of sour cream into which you have already stirred a tablespoonful of flour.

KALBSVÖGERLN
(Rolled stuffed Escallopes of veal — for 10 Escallopes)

1.) Allow one Escallope for each person and beat well. On each Escallope put a strip of bacon, one strip of pickled cucumber, one strip of raw carrot, salt and pepper, and roll the Escallope as you would a Swiss roll (along the fibres of the meat, not across).
Secure both ends with a tooth-pick or better still, tie firmly with thin string. Fry quickly until light brown on all sides and then simmer gently in a covered pan. If needed add a little water or pure soup.

2.) Prepare meat as in above recipe, only use a different stuffing: sliced mushrooms are put on the Escallopes, which are then rolled up and simmered together with more sliced mushrooms.

3.)

2 ozs onions = 1 medium onion	1 egg yolk
3 ozs fat = 6 tablespoons	1 tablespoon sour cream
½ lb minced veal	2 ozs butter = 4 tablespoons
	½ oz parsley = 1 tablespoon.

This time the filling consists of finely chopped onions, finely chopped parsley, and some minced veal. Fry the onion gently in a little butter, add the parsley and the minced veal, and the yolk of one egg. Mix well, add one teaspoon sour cream. When the mixture is cool, spread on the Escallopes. Roll up as in previous recipes and simmer gently on some finely chopped onions, which were fried golden brown before. If needed, add some clear soup to the gravy.

All these rolled veal Escallopes can be served with a gravy "naturel" or you can thicken it by stirring in a little flour and (or) add a little sour cream. Rice and noodles are best served with the Kalbsvögernl, which literally means "veal birds" because they look like little birds trussed for roasting.

EGGS IN THEIR NEST (Eier im Nest)

Allow 1 Escallope and 1 egg per person. Trim and beat Escallopes as usual, then put one hard boiled egg into the middle, fold meat around it, and secure with tooth-pick. Fry on all sides, then simmer slowly and add some sliced mushrooms. When the meat is done, take out of saucepan, remove tooth-picks and cut the veal rolls in half. Thicken the mushroom sauce with a little milk and flour or cream and flour. Place gravy in shallow serving dish and put veal rolls into it, with the egg showing. Serve with rice.

RAGOUT OF VEAL (Eingemachtes Kalbfleisch)

1 lb of veal	4 ozs mushrooms (about
2 ozs butter = 4 tablespoons	4 medium sized)
1 cup milk	3 carrots
1½ cups flour	½ package or tin of small peas
1 small cauliflower	1 egg yolk
	pinch of nutmeg

Cut the veal into cubes, and fry in 1 oz of butter, add the finely cut carrots and mushrooms, simmer for a few minutes, then cover with water. When boiling, add the cauliflower which you have broken into little sprigs and the green peas. When the meat is tender, add the milk into which the flour has been stirred and simmer for another five minutes. Now add the rest of the butter and the finely chopped parsley. Serve with small Bröselknodel (bread-crumb dumplings) or rice (see under Beilagen).

N o t e : This recipe can also be varied, and vegetables in season can be used. For instance, mushrooms only, cauliflower only, asparagus tips only or root of celery, carrots and peas, or carrots and peas only, or peas and asparagus, and so on.

STEWED MEAT AND RICE OR SAVOURY RICE WITH MEAT (Reisfleisch)

1½ lbs veal	1 teaspoonful paprika
½ lb rice = 2 cups	3 tablespoons oil

Cut the meat into cubes and chop the onions. Fry the onions golden brown in the oil, add the paprika and the meat, salt and simmer until the meat is half done. Now add the washed rice, and so much water that rice and meat are covered one finger high. Simmer over a very low flame. Serve sprinkled with grated cheese and a green salad.

N o t e : When in season, strips of green paprika and 1 or 2 peeled tomatoes can be added to the rice.

GULYAS

2 lbs veal	¼ pint sour cream
1 lb onions	1 teaspoon paprika
1 tablespoon flour	1 spoon tomato purée (optional)

Chop the onions and fry until golden brown. Then add the paprika and the meat which you have cut into cubes. Fry meat on all sides, add the salt, then simmer slowly on a low flame (adding a little water if necessary). When meat is soft, which will take about 1 hour, stir in the cream, which has been previously mixed with the flour. 1 spoon of tomato purée can now be added if liked, also another teaspoon of paprika, if the gulyas is too light. Simmer for a few more minutes. Nockerln (see under Beilagen), noodles, maccaroni or rice taste good with it.

I   STUFFED BREAST OF VEAL (Gefüllte Kalbsbrust)

2½ bread rolls (white)	1 tablespoon breadcrumbs
1½ ozs butter = 3 tablespoons	2 lbs veal
1 egg	1 teaspoon chopped parsley
2 tablespoons milk	

Take the rind of the rolls, dice, and put into a bowl with the milk. When soft, add the egg, the melted butter, salt, a pinch of nutmeg, the parsley and breadcrumbs. Clean the meat, loosen the rib-bones (but leave them in the meat). Make a pocket by making an incision with a sharp pointed knife between ribs and meat. Into this insert the stuffing and sew up the opening. Salt and pepper the meat, place in roasting tin, add a little water and a lump of butter. Put into heated oven and roast slowly, very slowly as the meat tears easily when done too quickly, and then the stuffing is in danger of falling out. Baste frequently, and before serving brush with fresh butter. To get a good color, it is a good trick to rub the meat with a little paprika before putting it into the oven. Serve with Risi-pisi (see under Beilagen), various salads or spring vegetables.

II   STUFFED BREAST OF VEAL (Gefüllte Kalbsbrust)

Is made in the same way, except that a small chopped onion and 4—5 small chopped mushrooms are fried slightly and added to the stuffing.

Beef

BOILED BEEF

was the main and most important part of the Austrian kitchen up to World War I. It had to be, because beef broth was eaten almost daily, and you can find under Soups some of the 100 ways in which you can ring the changes. In the smaller homes, beef was eaten as a main course, with vegetables and potatoes, and again, there are many sauces (see under Sauces) both cold and warm which give it a "new face" at each different serving. In the wealthier households it was served as "black meat", a second course between the soup and the roast. I have found that boiled beef is one of the things, almost like milk, eggs, bread and butter, which you can eat daily — more than you can do with roasts or fowl! You could try and cook a large piece of boiling beef (the larger the piece the better the soup) and have it for two or three days, you can also find recipes for using it cold.

Incidentally, boiled beef was the late Emperor Franz Joseph's favorite dish, he ate it almost daily too. How do I know? I thought you might be interested, so I contacted a very old man by the name of Lorenz Höferl, who lives outside Vienna, and who was his last valet. He was 37 years in the Imperial service and told me that the Emperor's taste was very frugal compared with his foodloving

The Emperor in his carriage

subjects! For breakfast he had tea with two rolls and butter and maybe a few biscuits. For lunch, boiled beef or Faschiertes, another simple dish that he was very fond of; and unless there was an official dinner, he never took supper, but had his last meal at 5 o'clock, consisting of coffee and Guglhupf (see under Cakes). No wonder he kept his trim figure into his very old age, as you can see from his pictures! At the official Court dinner parties, guests often used to get up hungry, he ate so little and so quickly, that the plates were removed before the guests had a chance to taste more than a mouthful, and sometimes not even that, as of course everybody had to stop when the Emperor did!

For the preparation of Boiled Beef see under "Soups": White Beef broth. Except in this case, the meat is put into the boiling soup to retain all its flavour. Perhaps I should mention here and now, in case of misunderstanding, that with the preparation of boiled beef it forms a dual service — at one and the same time, you obtain a soup a n d a meat course. According to taste, a lean or fat piece of boiling beef is used. When the meat is tender, it is sliced and served on a platter, covered with a little clear strained soup. For garnishing, see "Essentials" under Sauces. Any vegetable or salad can be served with this in addition to potatoes.

Now we come to one of our most famous specialities, which is an inheritance from our main fellow country in the old Monarchy — Hungary. There are two secrets important to know, and which are the making of every Gulyas: a) that you must use the same weight of onions as you use of meat and b) that it tastes even better warmed up, and the more (times) the merrier!

BEEFGULYAS (Rindsgulyas)

2 lbs beef	½ cup oil or
2 lbs onions	5 ozs lard = ½ cup
1½ tablespoons paprika	1 teaspoon vinegar
1½ tablespoons tomato purée	1 pinch marjoram

Fry the sliced onions in hot fat till golden brown, add the paprika and stir well; add the meat, cover, and let it simmer for a few minutes. Stir, so that it doesn't get too brown, add a few tablespoons of water and the tomato purée, 1 teaspoon salt, the vinegar and marjoram. Cover the saucepan and simmer very, very gently, adding water only in very small quantities as it becomes necessary. If more gravy is wanted, add a tablespoonful of flour, which you have mixed with water, and simmer for a few minutes, then add more water. But a Gulyas naturel without any flour is of course the real thing and also the best. Serve with boiled potatoes, Nockerl, Noodles or dumplings. A very good way to eat a Gulyas is just with a fresh and crisp roll. Try it! This, incididentally, is the way the small Gulyas was eaten by our grandfathers for their "elevenses" or "brunch".

GIPSY GULYAS (Zigeunergulyas)

Is made the same way as the above, only three kinds of meat are used: Beef, mutton and pork. It is made so that the beef is put in first, is simmered for ten minutes, then the mutton is added, and after ten more minutes, the pork. Then proceed as in the above recipe. Serve also with potatoes, noodles etc.

19

ZNAIM GULYAS (Znaimer Gulyas)

Znaim is a most charming, small town in Moravia, which also was a part of the Austro-Hungarian Monarchy, and is now Czechoslovakia.

It is a normal Beefgulyas to which you add two dill pickles (cucumber) cut like a fan for each person.

For more fancy trimmings for the Gulyas, you can use either of the following:

Beefgulyas, served with fried eggs, one to each person.

Beefgulyas, served with one hard boiled egg for each person.

Beefgulyas, served with one cut up Frankfurter for each person.

Strips of green or red paprika can also be cooked in the gravy.

Of the Gulyas family, you will also find other recipes: Veal gulyas, pork gulyas, gulyas soup, gulyasstrudel and potato gulyas.

VIENNA ROAST (Wiener Rostbraten)

3—4 beefsteaks cut to half an inch thickness
1 tablespoon lard or oil

1 tablespoon chopped onions to each steak

Trim the fat from the beefsteaks and make incisions with knife all around, beat well. Heat the lard in the frying pan, put the steaks in and fry quickly on both sides. Then lower the flame, add one tablespoon of chopped onions to each steak, fry on low flame until meat is done, then lift out and keep hot. Now continue to fry onions until golden brown, add a tablespoon of butter, stir, add a cup of clear beef broth. Bring to the boil and pour quickly over steaks. Serve at once, best with boiled potatoes which are fried with onions. (See recipe under Beilagen.)

Now a few recipes for **fillets of beef**. To improve their flavour, please treat them the following way:
Put them into a plate, sprinkle with pepper and some sprigs of parsley and cover with oil. Cover with another plate and leave for a few hours, and you will find that they are not only more tender, but actually tastier.

ROAST A LA ESZTERHAZY (Eszterhazy-Rostbraten)

The Eszterhazys are one of the oldest Autro-Hungarian aristocratic families. The Duke of Eszterhazy who lived in the Eighteenth century was the great benefactor of Josef Haydn, who was in the ducal employ for years, and there wrote some of his most beautiful music. The Eszterhazys were always linked with the Austrian history of music, Beethoven and Schubert performed many of their masterpieces for the first time at their soirées.
Now to return to more prosaic feats of the Dukes of Eszterhazy: they gave their name to this delicious beef dish:

5 fillets of beef
2 ozs flour = ½ cup
3 ozs fat = 6 tablespoons
salt and pepper

Sauce
2 tablespoons flour
½ pint sour cream = 1 cup
1 carrot
1 onion
salt
½ root Celery

21

Trim the fillets, make a few incisions all round, beat well, salt and pepper and dip into flour. One side only! Fry in hot fat on both sides (flour side first). Take the meat out when it is done and keep hot. To the fat in the saucepan add the flour which you brown, then add the sour cream, whisking well so that no lumps are formed. The vegetables must be diced meanwhile and sautéed in butter until tender. Serve the fillets on a deeper dish, cover with the sauce and put the vegetables on top. Potatoes are served with this.

ROLLS OF FILLETED BEEF (Rinds-Rouladen)

Fillets of beef are trimmed, beaten well, rubbed with pepper and salt, and rolled together. They can be either fried and served like this, or can be filled with either of the following mixtures:

1. *Minced beef, well seasoned*

2. *A mixture of minced pork and veal, well seasoned*

3. *A strip of carrot, a strip of dill pickle, a strip of bacon*

4. *½ a Frankfurter and a strip of bacon*

You can either fry the rolls on their own and thicken the gravy to a cream sauce (see recipe for Kalbsvögerl) or fry them on a bed of chopped onion and simmer until done. This is best served with noodles.

BEEF WITH ONIONS (Zwiebelfleisch)

1 lb beef
¾ lb onions
¼ lb lard = ½ cup
2 tablespoons flour
1 tablespoon vinegar

½ pint sour cream = 1 cup
1 cup beef broth or stock
Salt, pepper, chopped carraway seeds, half a teaspoonful marjoram

Fry the chopped onions golden brown in the hot fat. Pour 1 table-spoonful of vinegar over it, add the soup or stock. Now cut the meat into thin slices and add to the onions. Put in the marjoram, the carraway seeds, salt and pepper, then simmer until soft. Mix the flour with the sour cream, add to the meat, and simmer for another five minutes. Serve with Nockerln.

JOINT OF BEEF WITH BACON (Speckbraten)

3 lbs beef (roasting beef)	1 bayleaf
3 ozs bacon	1 pinch thyme
½ carrot	1 pinch nutmeg
½ onion	1 oz dark rye bread = 1 medium
pepper, salt	slice
20 black pepper corns	¼ pint red wine = ¼ cup

Trim the joint, beat well, make holes in it with a skewer (into the length of the joint). If the holes are not large enough, enlarge them with the end of a wooden cooking spoon. Now cut the bacon into long strips and push into the holes, again with the aid of the cooking spoon. Rub the meat with pepper and salt. Put into roasting pan together with the vegetables, which you have previously diced and fried slightly. Add a little water and slowly roast in the oven. Baste all the time, adding water or clear soup if necessary. If the vegetables get brown you must add a little more water. When the meat is done, remove the fat of the gravy, add the red wine, the pepper corns, the bayleaf, the thyme and also the bread which has been soaked in the red wine. Return to the oven and leave there for another five minutes. Put the vegetables and bread through a coarse sieve, add this to the gravy and serve the roast covered with the sauce. Noodles, Nockerl, rice or potatoes, all taste equally well with this.

ROAST OF BEEF WITH FRANKFURTERS
(Frankfurterbraten)

This is done in the same way, except that Frankfurters (skinned) are used instead of the bacon.

HARLEKINBRATEN

The same as Frankfurterbraten, only long strips of carrot, bacon or ham, and pickled cucumber are inserted into the joint, so that it gives the impression of coloured mosaic when cut. These three last recipes can also be made with roast veal.

Beefsteaks are not really an Austrian dish, and I expect you know more about them than I do. But let me give you a special recipe that may be new to you.

BEEFSTEAKS IN PASTRY

Make enough pastry so that you get two rounds, the size of your largest casserole (it should be one which you can bring to the table). Use your own favourite pastry recipe or one out of this book. Now cover the bottom of this casserole with the pastry. Peel the potatoes, cut into small slices and salt a little. The beefsteak should be the thickness of a finger, and should be fried in butter quickly on both sides. Flavour with salt and pepper. On the pastry in the casserole put a layer of potatoes, then one layer of beefsteaks, then potatoes again, and so on. The last layer should be potatoes. Put into a medium oven and leave there for two hours, basting the top layer all the time with butter. Of the remaining pastry, make a lid, baked separately, and then, before serving, cover the casserole. Serve with various salads, or a platter of mixed vegetables. (See under Vegetables in this book.)

Pork

BOILED LEG OF PORK (Gekochte Schweinsstelze)

1 hind leg of pork
1 medium head of green
 cabbage
1 medium head of white
 cabbage

20 small carrots
20 small potatoes
50 small onions (shallott onions)
 1 bayleaf and a few black pepper
 corns

Wash and salt the leg of pork (unskinned). Put in a large saucepan, cover with water, add the bayleaf and the peppercorns. Boil for 10 minutes, then add all the vegetables. The heads of cabbage should be quartered. When the meat is soft, take out of the stew, carve, put on a dish that is deep enough to hold part of the soup, cover with the vegetables and as much soup as it will take. The rest of the soup is served separately. Grated horseradish or horseradish sauce is served with this. There should not be too much soup, it should boil down while cooking and, if possible, nothing should be added.

GULYAS WITH SHREDDED CABBAGE
(Szegediner Gulyas oder Krautfleisch)
(Szegedin is a town in Hungary)

1 lb pork
1 lb shredded white cabbage
salt, pepper, paprika, carraway
 seeds

1/2 lb onions
2 dessertspoons fat
3 to 4 medium tomatoes
3 to 4 medium green peppers

Cut onion and fry golden brown, cut meat into cubes and fry over onions, slowly, and on all sides; but not too much, as there must not be a hard crust. Now the peeled tomatoes and the peppers which you have cut into strips are added. Stir well. Add the shredded cabbage and the seasonings. Simmer for an hour. If liked, 2 to 3 tablespoons of sour cream can be added when meat and

26

cabbage are tender just before serving. Tastes best with plain boiled potatoes.

STEWED AND SHREDDED CABBAGE WITH DICED PORK
(Krautfleisch)

Is made in the same way as the above recipe, only Sauerkraut is used instead of the cabbage and the green peppers and tomatoes are omitted. If liked, 2 teaspoons of paprika can be added.

GULYAS OF PORK (Schweinsgulyas)

Is prepared the same way as Kalbsgulyas.

SZEKELY GULYAS

1 lb pork ⎱ *both of the leg*	*1 lb Sauerkraut*
1 lb veal ⎰ *preferably*	*½ pint sour cream = ½ cup*
2 pairs Frankfurters	*½ lb onions*
½ cup tomato purée	*1 cup beef broth*

Chop and fry the onions, add the pork which you have cubed and when this is partly cooked, add the cubed pork. Now add the Sauerkraut, cover and simmer for half an hour. In a jug mix the tomato purée, the cream and the soup together with 2 tablespoons flour. Pour over the Sauerkraut, stir and simmer for 10 more minutes. Just before serving add the sliced Frankfurter and serve with Semmelknödel (see under Beilagen).

VIRGIN'S ROAST (Jungfernbraten)

Heaven alone knows the reason for this name, I've given you a literal translation. The only reason I can think of, is that it is supposed to come from a rather lean and young pig, but I really don't know if it must be virginal!

2 lbs lean roasting pork

1 medium sized onion

2 parsley roots

2 carrots

1 tablespoon fat

1 teaspoon chopped capers

1 teaspoon chopped parsley

salt, pepper, paprika, carraway seeds

Rub the meat with salt, pepper and paprika. Sprinkle with carraway seeds. Chop all vegetables and fry in a spoonful of fat. Then put into a roasting tin, which has a lid. Add the meat and very little water. Cover tin, put into oven, and cook slowly. Add water if needed. Just before the meat is tender, remove the lid. Leave for another five to ten minutes, enough for the meat to take on a little colour. Now take meat out, slice and keep hot. To the vegetables in the baking tin add one cup of sour cream, stir well, add the chopped parsley and the chopped capers, bring to the boil and pour over sliced meat.

ROAST PORK (Schweinsbraten)

2 lbs of a lean joint of pork   *1 clove garlic*
1 tablespoon mustard   *1 teaspoon carraway seeds*

Rub meat with crushed garlic, salt, pepper and the French mustard. Heat oven well, put meat into baking dish, add a little stock or water, cover and put into oven, the heat of which is now lowered. Baste frequently. If it is a fatter piece of pork, make a few incisions with a knife, about half an inch apart when the meat is half done. Now take the lid off and finish roasting. When meat is tender take out of pan, remove the fat from the gravy, add water or stock to the baking tin, bring to the boil, and cook lightly for a few moments. Serve gravy separately in gravy boat. Now there are several ways in which you can serve this pork. There is one group of pork lovers who will eat it with either rice or potatoes, stewed apples, any vegetable or any salad, even mayonnaise-salad. Then there are others who like it the way it is eaten in Bohemia and Moravia (Czechoslovakia), that is, with any dumplings (potato dumplings, bread dumplings, serviette dumplings) and white cabbage or Sauerkraut.

SAVORY RICE AND DICED MEAT (Reisfleisch)

Is made in the same way as Kalbsreisfleisch, only green peppers and peeled tomatoes are added.

WIENER SCHNITZEL

Made of Escallopes of pork are made the same way as Vealschnitzel.

CREAMED ESCALLOPES (Rahmschnitzel)
See under Veal

PARISERSCHNITZEL
See under Veal

NATURSCHNITZEL
See under Veal

Mutton and Lamb

You will perhaps be surprised that I am only giving you so few recipes for this meat, but it is eaten very seldom here in Austria.

SPRING LAMB (Gebackenes Lämmernes)

Can be prepared the same way as a Wiener Schnitzel, and this dish is usually eaten at Eastertime. It can also be prepared in the same way as "Eingemachtes Kalbfleisch". I know of course several other ways to prepare mutton, but these are mostly imported ones. But keeping in mind that this is a cookery book for our specialities only, I have only chosen those dishes which are really Austrian.

MUTTON WITH GREEN BEANS (Schöpsernes mit grünen Fisolen)

1 leg of mutton   *1 lb green beans*
1 lb potatoes   *1 large onion*

Cut the meat of the leg into regular pieces. Peel the potatoes and cut into thick slices. String the beans (I would advise you to use either fresh or frozen ones as the tinned variety don't have enough taste for this particular dish). Break the beans into pieces of 1 to 2 inches long, peel the onion and cut into thin slices. All these ingredients are flavoured well with paprika and salt. Now take a saucepan which has a lid. Spread the bottom fairly thickly with butter and spread one layer of the sliced onion on top of this. Then follow with a layer of meat, then of beans (putting a few dabs of butter on the beans). Now put on the potatoes, and again a little more butter. The potatoes should form the last layer. If you and your family fancy it, put a piece of garlic on top. Cover and simmer slowly for about 1½ hours.

STYRIAN MUTTON STEW (Steirisches Wurzelfleisch)

Styria is one of the nine provinces of Austria and, I think, one of the loveliest. It has high mountains and beautiful hills, it has lakes and woods and it's capital is the old historic town of Graz.

2 lbs shoulder of mutton	½ medium sized onion
½ carrot	4 tablespoons fat
½ parsley root	black peppercorn
½ small root of celery	pinch of thyme
1 lb potatoes	1 teaspoon vinegar

Cut the meat into cubes and put into a saucepan with the vegetables (cut into small pieces). Add the spices. Cover with water, bring to the boil and simmer until half tender. Now add the peeled potatoes which you have halved or quartered according to size.

Ground Beef and Pork, mixed

I   **MEAT LOAF (Faschierter Braten)**

1 lb ground beef
1 lb ground pork
3 white rolls
1 egg
2 ozs bacon fat = 2 tablespoons
salt and pepper
1 oz chopped parsley = 2 table-
spoons

2 ozs chopped onion = 1 medium
sized
1 oz lard = 1 tablespoon
(for frying onion)
2 ozs flour = ½ cup
2 ozs lard (for melting) = 2 table-
spoons
1 pinch marjoram

See that the beef is ground from a lean piece, while the pork can be fat. In a bowl, mix the meat with the rolls (previously soaked in a little milk and water and which have been squeezed well and put through the mincer). Add the chopped bacon, the chopped parsley, the chopped and fried onion, the egg, salt and pepper. Mix all ingredients well, and make into a loaf shape with some bread crumbs in a greased loaf pan or a shallow baking dish. Now heat the two ounces of lard, pour over the loaf, and put into a moderately hot oven. Add a little soup or stock after a few minutes, baste frequently and bake for 1½ hours. If liked, you can add a cup of sour cream to the gravy after you have spooned off the surplus fat, and return to the oven for a few more minutes. It is served with various salads, creamed potatoes, various vegetables.

II   **HUNTER'S MEAT LOAF (Jägerbraten)**

The same ingredients as in the meat loaf, but when forming
the loaf, use only half of the mixture, and retain the other.
On the first half which you have put in the baking tin in the
shape of half a loaf (lengthways) put hard boiled eggs and pickled cucumbers (as many as possible) on top and cover with the rest
of the meat. Form into a loaf and roast in the usual way.

III   **MEAT LOAF**

Is made in the same way as Jägerbraten, except that Frankfurters
are substituted for the hard boiled eggs and cucumbers.

IV   **MEAT LOAF**

Again, the same procedure, but this time the filling consists
of scrambled eggs.

You can also mix Meat Loaf Nos. 3 and 4 and put Frankfurters in
the middle of the scrambled eggs.

The meat loaves are all extremely tasty when eaten cold, especially
the plain one with potato salad.

MEAT BALLS (Fleischlaberln)

Are made from the same mixture as the meat loaf, and moulded into sizes a little smaller than a tennis ball, and then pressed flat. There are many alternative ways of making these.

1.) Fry in hot fat and serve with potatoes, vegetables and any salad.

2.) Fry onions golden brown, add a little flour, let this become brown, add stock, bring to the boil, turn the flame low, put the meat balls in, and simmer in the sauce until they are done.

3.) Fry the meat balls on both sides, take out ot the pan, spoon of the surplus fat, add a little stock, and when this boils, add one cup of sour cream into which you have stirred one table-spoon of flour. Simmer for a few minutes, and return the meat balls to this sauce. Serve with noodles, spaghetti or Nockerl.

4.) Make a tomato sauce as given in "ESSENTIALS" and stew the meat balls in it. Serve with rice.

STUFFED TOMATOES (Gefüllte Paradeiser)

10 Tomatoes
Ground meat mixture as before
2 ozs grated cheese = 5 table-spoons

1 oz bread crumbs = 2½ table-spoons
2½ ozs butter = 6 tablespoons

Take good sized tomatoes, cut off the end and take seeds out with a spoon carefully. (This can be used for tomato soup.) Put stuffing into tomatoes and put them side by side into a buttered baking dish. Sprinkle with grated cheese and breadcrumbs, melt the butter, pour over tomatoes and put for 10 minutes into hot oven.

STUFFED GREEN PEPPERS (Gefüllte Paprika)

1.) *10 Paprika*   *Tomato sauce as in "Essentials".*
½ the mixture of meat loaf
No. 1

Wash the paprika, cut off the top, take out the seeds and parboil them slightly. Now stuff them with the ground meat mixture and simmer for one hour in the tomato sauce. Serve with rice.

2.) Prepare the mixture as in No. 1 but instead of adding the white rolls, add ¾ cup of boiled rice. Now stuff the paprika in the same way and fry them in hot fat on all sides in two tablespoons of oil. When they are nicely brown, add 2 lbs of peeled and cut tomatoes, 1 teaspoon of sugar, ½ a teaspoon of salt and 1 teaspoon of vinegar. Simmer until paprikas are soft.

STUFFED KOHLRABI (Gefüllte Kohlrabi)

10 Kohlrabi
½ the meat mixture as in
    meatloaf 1

       Sauce
2 ozs butter = ¼ cup
2 ozs flour = ½ cup

½ oz chopped parsley = 1 table-
    spoon

the finely chopped inner part of a
Kohlrabi which you have taken out,
the chopped tender leaves of the
Kohlrabi if it has any.

Peel the Kohlrabi, take off the top part and with a sharp knife take out as much as you can of the inside. The Kohlrabi shells which you now have, are parboiled in salted water. Now fill them with the ground meat mixture, put into a buttered casserole, cover with 3 tablespoons of stock or water and cook slowly for about ½ an hour or until Kohlrabi are tender.

Serve covered with the sauce, prepared as follows:

Melt the butter, add the flour (be careful that it doesn't get too brown), add to this the chopped inside of a Kohlrabi which you have simmered in a little water, which shouldn't be strained off. Then add the parsley, salt and pepper, bring to the boil, simmer for five minutes and pour over Kohlrabi.

STUFFED CUCUMBERS (Gefüllte frische Gurken)

3 large cucumbers
The same quantity of meat mixture as before

Sauce
3 ozs butter = $^6/_7$ tablespoons
2 ozs flour = 1/2 cup

1 oz chopped onions = 1 tablespoon
1 oz chopped parsley = 2 tablespoons
2 ozs chopped dill = 4 tablespoons
1 1/2 tablespoons of vinegar
1/2 cup sour cream
salt and paprika

Cut off both ends of the cucumber, peel, and take out the seeds (make incisions round the seeds with sharp pointed knife at both ends as far down as possible, then push out seeds with the end of wooden spoon). For pushing in the stuffing also use the end of a wooden spoon.

Sauce:

Melt the butter, add the onions, turn a few times, they should not take on any colour, add the flour, the parsley and 1 pint of water; salt, paprika, the vinegar mixed with the cream, the dill and bring to the boil. Turn flame low, add the cucumber and simmer until these are soft.

STUFFED CABBAGE ROLLS (Krautwürstel)

Half of the original meat loaf 1 mixture.
1 white cabbage.

1.) Take off the large leaves of a head of white cabbage, be careful not to break them. Take out the stalk if this is too coarse, but see that the leaves remain whole. Parboil them and spread them with the stuffing. Roll up, fold over the ends, and secure with two tooth picks.

In a casserole put 2 tablespoons of oil and fry the cabbage rolls on all sides until dark brown. Add 1 pint of water or stock and simmer until tender. Serve with boiled potatoes.

2.) Make in the same way, adding one cup of sour cream (into which you have stirred one tablespoon of flour) to the gravy and simmer for five more minutes.

3.) Again the same as 1. but this time, the rest of the cabbage is shredded and a buttered casserole is filled with the cabbage rolls, then the shredded cabbage, then cabbage rolls again, and so on. Top with sour cream and put into a medium hot oven. Leave there for about an hour, adding a little more sour cream from time to time.

4.) Repeat as for 3. only using Sauerkraut instead of the shredded cabbage.

5.) Prepare Sauerkraut naturel, you will find the recipe in this book under Vegetables. Put the rolls into this and simmer until they are soft.

N o t e : Strips of bacon can be put around the cabbage rolls in those recipes where they are fried first.

The remains of the cabbage, that is, the inner part, when the leaves get too small for rolls, can be used for cabbage salad, stewed cabbage or Krautfleckerln. Recipes for all of these are in this book.

Organ meats
(Innereien)
Brains

BRAINS A LA WIENER SCHNITZEL (Gebackenes Hirn)

If possible, use calf's brains for this recipe. Allow one brain for 2 persons. For cleaning the brain, boil 2 cups of water with 1 tablespoon of vinegar. Add a pinch of salt. Parboil the brains for a few minutes, strain, and skin. Leave to cool and then cut into thick slices which are then dipped into flour, egg and breadcrumbs, as with a Schnitzel. Fry in hot fat, and serve with salads.

FRIED BRAINS (Geröstetes Hirn)

3 veal or beef brains (about 2 lbs)	1 oz chopped onion = 2 tablespoons
⅓ cup of fat	pepper and salt
	1 teaspoon chopped parsley

Wash and skin the brains (this is easier if you have left them in warm water for a few minutes). Chop as well as you can on a board. Fry the chopped onions golden brown, add the brains, stir well. Before serving, add salt, pepper and the chopped parsley. Serve hot on hot buttered toast as an entrée.

FRIED BRAINS WITH EGG (Hirn mit Ei)

The same as the above recipe, except that 4 beaten eggs are added to the mixture after the brain is cooked. Cook until eggs are set. Lamb's and pig's brain can be used the same way.

BRAIN GNOCCHI (Hirnnockerln)

1 knob of butter (size of an egg)
1 brain (veal)
salt, pepper

1 teaspoon chopped parsley
breadcrumbs (as much as the mixture will take)

Put the butter into a basin, cream well, add the egg, stir well. Now add the cleaned brains and continue to stir for five minutes. Salt, pepper and the finely chopped parsley are added and as many breadcrumbs to get a smooth mixture. Leave to stand for one and half hours. Now try the mixture and, if necessary, add some more breadcrumbs. You should be able to form Nockerln with the help of a tablespoon. Dip your spoon into clear soup, which should boil slowly. Drop the Nockerln into it, one by one. They are cooked for about five to eight minutes and are served as an entrée on a bed of creamed spinach.

BRAINPUDDING (Hirnpudding)

1 large calf's brain
4 ozs butter = 8 tablespoons or
½ cup
4 eggs
¼ lb green cooked peas
¼ lb sliced cooked mushrooms
1 small onion

1 teaspoon finely chopped parsley

B e c h a m é l
2 ozs flour = 1 cup
1 small cup cream
2 ozs butter = 5 tablespoons

Prepare the Bechamél (as in "Essentials") and leave to cool. Now add the 4 ozs butter and the 4 egg yolks. Stir well.
Fry the chopped onion until golden brown, add the chopped brain and the chopped parsley. Add this to the Bechamél mixture, stir well. Now add the cooked green peas and mushrooms. Finally, fold in carefully the 4 egg whites which you have beaten stiffly. Butter and flour a pudding basin, fill in the brain mixture, cover and put into boiling water. Be careful that no water can get into it. Steam for an hour, but not too quickly. Serve with a tomato sauce or a green salad as an entrée or with potatoes or rice as a main dish.

PANCAKES WITH BRAIN FILLINGS (Hirnpalatschinken)

1 oz butter = 2½ tablespoons *1 veal brain*
1 pinch chopped parsley *1 tablespoon white wine or cooking*
salt and pepper *sherry*

These are only the ingredients for the filling.
Prepare the pancakes in your usual way (or using my recipe) and
then fill with the brain mixture. Fry the chopped brains, add a
tablespoon of wine, spread on pancakes and roll together. Serve
hot with a green salad as an entrée or light main dish.

BRAINS ON TOAST (Hirnpofesen)

10 small pieces of toast *2 cups or 1 pint of milk mixed*
1 veal brain *with 1 egg*
1 small onion *2 eggs*
½ teaspoon parsley *breadcrumbs for coating*
  1 oz fat = 1 tablespoon

Prepare the brains and cook as in "Brains with Egg". The toast is
prepared in the following way. Beat the egg with the milk and soak
the bread slices for a few minutes. Dip into the breadcrumbs and
fry crisply on both sides. Spread with the brain mixture, top with
another slice of toast and serve hot. This is good used as hot ca-
napés for cocktails or served as an entrée on a bed of spinach.

Liver

TYROLEAN LIVER (Tiroler Leber)

I am sure there is no need for me to tell you much about the Tyrol. I think it must be the best known of all Austrian provinces to travellers. So well known in fact, that everything slightly resembling a "Dirndl" (the name for our colourful peasant costume) is called tyrolean, even if it comes from one of the other provinces. The capital of Tyrol is Innsbruck, and it is certainly one of the most beautiful parts of Austria — it has also produced most of our ace skiers.

2 lbs liver (calf's for preference)	3 tablespoons sour cream
½ oz flour = 1½ tablespoons	½ oz capers = 1 teaspoon
3 ozs fat = 6 tablespoons	1 tablespoon vinegar
2 ozs onions = 4 tablespoons	1½ cups soup or water
	salt

Cut the liver into slices about ¼ of an inch thick, put into flour on one side. Now fry on both sides (flour side first) and keep hot. In the same fat, fry onion golden brown, add the flour, the water and the cream. Stir well to avoid lumps forming. Add the chopped capers, and the vinegar, bring to the boil, simmer slowly and 5 minutes before serving, add the liver and just before you serve, the salt. Serve with Nockerln, rice or Erdaepfelschmarren (see Beilagen).

LIVERGULYAS (Lebergulyas)

Is made the same way as Rindsgulyas. Be careful not to put the salt in until you serve. Liver can also be sliced and made the same way as Wiener Schnitzel, it is then called Gebackene Leber. Again, be careful with the salt, as it hardens the liver. The best way is to salt at the table. For livergulyas, any kind of liver can be used. For Wiener Schnitzel, only calf's liver.

FRIED LIVER WITH ONIONS (Geröstete Leber)

1 lb liver	*1 pinch marjoram*
3 ozs = 6 tablespoons	*1 cup of water or stock*
3 ozs onions = 5 tablespoons	*salt, pepper*

Cut the liver into small pieces, slice the onion and fry golden brown. Add the liver to the onion, fry for about eight minutes, stirring occasionally. Now add the marjoram and 1 cup of soup or water. Salt and pepper are added just before serving.

Eat with Nockerln, rice or Erdäpfelschmarren (see under Beilagen).

LIVER PREPARED AS GAME (Leber auf Wildart zubereitet)

2 lbs calf's liver	*1 cup cream*
3 ozs fat = 6 tablespoons	*5 juniper berries*
1 oz flour = 3 tablespoons	

Cut the liver into thick slices, put into flour and fry on both sides. Take out and keep hot. Add one cup of clear soup to the frying pan together with the juniper berries. Bring to the boil and simmer for a few minutes. Now add the sour cream into which you have stirred the flour, simmer for a few more minutes, take out the berries and pour over the liver. Tastes best with maccaroni or any other members of the "pasta" family.

LIVERGNOCCHI (Lebernockerln)

½ lb liver	*2 rolls (soaked in clear broth)*
1 small onion	*a few breadcrumbs*

The rolls have been soaked in the stock and squeezed dry.
Now put the liver through the mincer and afterwards, the rolls.
The fried onion and parsley are also put through the mincer.

To this mixture, add enough breadcrumbs to enable you to form a Nockerl with a tablespoon. Bring some water to the boil and try one Nockerl first. If the mixture stays together you can continue with the others. To make the mixture firmer, add a few more bread-crumbs; to make it softer, add a drop of milk. These Nockerln can be either served in a clear soup, or they should be placed in a deep serving dish and covered with a Bechamél, into which you have put a few small green peas and sliced mushrooms. In this case, serve with rice as a main dish, or as an entrée, without anything.

KIDNEYS (Nierndln)

Kidneys should be put into a mixture of milk and water or vinegar and water for a few hours. The white part should be taken out. Pig's kidneys are mostly used, but veal and mutton kidneys can be treated the same way.

KIDNEYS AND BRAINS (Nierndln mit Hirn)

5 pig's kidneys	*3 ozs fat = 6 tablespoons*
3 pig's brains	*salt, pepper, paprika*
3 ozs onion = 5 tablespoons	*a pinch of marjoram*

Slice the kidneys and chop the brains. Cut the onions and fry in the fat, adding the kidneys which you then fry for five minutes. Stir occasionally and add the brains. Now salt and pepper and cook until the brains are done. Serve with rice or Erdäpfelschmarren (see under Beilagen).

KIDNEYS AND ONIONS (Geröstete Nierndln)

Are prepared the same way as liver and onions.

VEAL-TONGUE (Kalbszunge)

2 *veal tongues*	1 *onion*
5 *black peppercorns*	1 *carrot*
1 *bayleaf*	

Put the vegetables and the tongue into a saucepan, cover with water, add salt and boil until the tongues are soft. Take out the tongue and peel off the hard outer skin. Now cut into slices and put into a sauce made of a Bechamél with any vegetables in season. Preferably green peas and mushrooms or cauliflower. For the Bechamél, use the water in which you have cooked the tongue. Serve with Bröselknödel. (See under Beilagen.)

PORK-TONGUE (Schweinszunge)

3 *pork tongues*	3 *carrots*
bayleaf	2 *onions*
carraway seeds	1 *root of celery*
	3 to 4 *large potatoes*

Cook the tongue in salted water to which you have added the bayleaf and peppercorns. When the tongue is done, take out of the water, peel and cut into slices. To the water add now the vegetables which you have cut into long, fairly thick sticks.

OX-TONGUE (Rindszunge)

Either cured or smoked are just cooked in water without the addition of salt, as they are usually very salty. They are peeled, sliced and served hot, mostly with creamed potatoes, or potato purée or a purée of dried yellow or green split peas.

Poultry and Game

The most typically Austrian, or rather Viennese dish in poultry, is the "Backhendl" (Spring chicken made as Wiener Schnitzel). In prosperous Regency days, what we call the Biedermeier — the protruding stomach of a portly Gentleman — would be called: a "Backhendlfriedhof!" (Fried chicken cemetary!). Somewhat macabre, however true! Nowadays, it is the only warm dish that you get at our famous Heurigen, the vineyards where you sit in gardens and sample the new wine, and where more often only cold cuts are eaten.

CHICKEN A LA WIENER SCHNITZEL (Backhendl)
(SOUTHERN FRIED CHICKEN)

Allow half a spring chicken to each person, or even a whole one if they are very small. Halve and quarter them, according to size, dip into flour, egg and breadcrumbs and fry. Serve hot with various salads. The liver and the cleaned stomach are also coated and fried.

I   CREAMED PAPRIKACHICKEN (Paprikahuhn)

1 large roasting chicken	*1 lb onions*
5 ozs fat = ³/₄ cup	*1 teaspoon paprika*
½ pint sour cream = ½ cup	*3 teaspoons tomato purée*

Cut the chicken into medium sized pieces. Fry the chopped onions in the fat, add the paprika, then the chicken. Fry chicken on all sides. Now add the tomato purée and a little water, salt. Simmer until meat is tender, on a low flame with the lid on. Now add the cream into which you have stirred 1 oz flour. Simmer for a few minutes. Serve with Nockerl or any pasta.

II

This can be made of a boiling chicken. Prepare as in the following recipe. When chicken is done, take out of soup, cut into convenient pieces. Now prepare the following sauce: Chop 1 lb onions, fry in 4 ozs fat, add two teaspoons of paprika, 1 tablespoon of tomato purée and add some chicken soup, sufficient for all the chicken which you now put in. Mix ½ pint of sour cream with 1 oz of flour, mix into gravy, simmer for a few more minutes. In this recipe, you have nearly all the soup left for separate use, and it is also a good way to prepare an old fowl.

BOILED CHICKEN (Suppenhuhn)

1 large boiling fowl	*parsley (the green and the root),*
about 1 lb of mixed soup vege-	*celeryroot.*
tables: carrot, onion or leek,	

Put the chicken (whole or cut into half) into a large saucepan, also the stomach and the liver, together with the cut vegetables. Cover well with water, salt and bring to the boil. Simmer until chicken is done. Take the chicken out of the soup, strain vegetables, and cook some thin vermicelli in the soup. The chicken is cut into smallish pieces, or if preferred, the meat only is taken off. Now return this to the soup, which is served as a hot-pot.

MUSHROOM-CHICKEN (Eingemachtes Huhn mit Schwämmen)

1 frying chicken   *1 oz butter = 6 tablespoons*
2 ozs mushrooms   *1 oz flour = 3 tablespoons*

Cut the chicken into convenient pieces. Fry in the butter on all sides, now add the sliced mushrooms, add a little water, salt and simmer under cover until meat is tender. Now mix the flour with ½ cup of sweet cream, and add this to the chicken; simmer a few minutes longer and serve with rice or Bröselknödel (see under Beilagen).

M u s h r o o m c h i c k e n can also be prepared with a boiling fowl which is prepared in the same way as the recipe No. 2 for Paprikachicken. In this case, the mushrooms are sautéed separately, some chicken soup is added, then the cream together with the flour and finally, the chicken.

In the same way, a boiling fowl can be prepared with other vegetables:

1. cauliflower
2. peas and carrots
3. asparagus
4. mixed vegetables. Chopped parsley can be added to all of these.

CHICKEN-RICE (Hühnerreis)

The meat is taken off a boiled fowl and together with the liver, is cut into small pieces. Now you cook 1 lb of rice. Fry first in 3 ozs butter, then add 3 cups of chickensoup, 1 oz of sliced mushrooms, 10 ozs of cooked green peas. When rice is done, mix the chicken meat with it and serve with salad and grated cheese.

SADDLE OF VENISON (Rehrücken)

1 saddle of venison　　　　　*crushed juniperberries*
4 ozs baconstrips (fat)　　　*pepper, salt*
1 oz fat for the baking dish =
　2 tablespoons

Trim and skin the saddle. Rub with pepper, salt and the crushed juniperberries. Make incisions with pointed knife, inserting the strips of bacon. Grease the baking dish, put meat into it, add a little water or stock, and roast for about an hour, basting very frequently, and adding a little hot soup or stock if it becomes necessary. If you cover the meat with thin bacon slices at the beginning, and later remove when they become brown, it will prevent the meat from getting too dry. But this is optional, and if it is laced with enough bacon fat inside, and is basted frequently, it will preserve its juicy texture. Serve with potato croquettes and cranberry jelly.

Saddle of Hare and Leg of Venison can be made in the same way.

SADDLE OF VENISON IN CREAM SAUCE
(Rehrücken in Rahmsauce)

The above method is repeated, except that the gravy is cleared of all superfluous fat. When the meat is taken out, a cup of sour cream to which you have added one tablespoon of flour and a teaspoon of redcurrant jelly is mixed with the gravy, simmered for a few seconds and then served separately, or poured over the meat. Serve with noodles, rice, croquettes or Semmelknödel and cranberry sauce. (Again Saddle of Hare and Leg or Loin of Venison can be prepared this way.)

LEG AND LOIN OF VENISON IN CREAM SAUCE
(Rehschlögel in Rahmsauce)

1 medium sized onion
2 carrots
½ root celery
french mustard
stock

1 pint sour cream
2 bayleaves
a little grated nutmeg
1 cup of red wine

Skin and trim the meat. Rub with crushed juniper berries, pepper and salt. Shred the vegetables, and fry in two tablespoons of fat. Add the meat (as a whole) to this and fry until nicely browned on all sides. Then place in a large casserole (one with a lid) with the vegetables, the bayleaves, thyme, the nutmeg and about two cups of stock. Add the french mustard and a little grated orange peel. Simmer until meat is tender, under cover of course. Take meat out, and keep hot. To finish the sauce, add a teaspoon of french mustard, a teaspoon of redcurrant jelly and the red wine. Finally, the sour cream (1 pint) into which you have stirred a tablespoon of flour. Serve the meat sliced with rice or noodles, Semmelknödel and cranberry jelly. This way also, the lesser parts of the venison can be prepared. For an alternative method, see the following recipe.

MARINATED VENISON, HARE OR RABBIT (Gebeiztes Wild)

This is an excellent way to prepare the lesser parts of all kinds of venison or to prepare rabbit. It is so tasty that at times when no game is available, a piece of beef can be prepared this way.
The meat is washed, divided into convenient parts and placed into a large bowl.

2 pints water	2 tablespoons flour
3 ozs parsley root	½ pint vinegar = ½ cup
10 black peppercorns	3 ozs carrot
10 juniper berries	1½ ozs celery
4 bayleaves, a sprig of thyme, salt	½ pint sour cream

Parboil the vegetables with the seasonings in the water with the vinegar (for about 10 minutes). Cool. Now pour over meat, cover the bowl and let it stand overnight. The meat must be completely covered with the liquid. The next day, simmer everything until meat is tender, then remove meat, and put the sauce through a sieve. Bring to the boil once more, and add ½ pint of sour cream into which you have stirred 2 tablespoons of flour. Simmer for a few more minutes, add a knob of butter, return the meat to the sauce and serve with Noodles or dumplings. If a thicker sauce is required, an "Einbrenn" (see under "Essentials") can be added, the cream is then added without any flour.

Fish

This will be quite a short chapter, understandably so, for as you know, we have no sea! Did you know that Shakespeare thought we had? In "A Winter's Tale" he describes Bohemia (which was then part of Austria) as lying on the sea! That shows how very unimportant geographical knowledge can be sometimes! But somehow the Austrian housewives are very much aware of the fact that the sea is a considerable distance away, and n o t so much aware that with deep freezing and modern transport this is not quite as far as it used to be. Be that as it may, they show a certain reluctance over sea food, and as you are probably more knowledgeable, I shall only give you recipes for the fish that we have in our own lakes and rivers.

Foremost, there is Carp, which is brought from the Danube or the lakes:

BREADED CARP (Gebackener Karpfen)

It is cleaned, washed, dried and treated the usual way. Be careful that the frying pan is really hot as fish sticks so easily. Serve with salad.

GYPSY CARP (Zigeunerkarpfen)

2 lbs carp	¼ pint of sour cream = ¼ cup
½ lb onions	salt
½ oz of bacon	paprika

Cut the fish into convenient portions. Salt well and leave for ½ an hour. Butter a fireproof dish, and put in a layer of fish. Then sprinkle with the onions which you have fried in the cubed bacon and paprika. Continue with another layer of fish, then onions, and so on. Pour half of the cream over it and put into a hot oven until the fish is cooked. Now pour the remaining cream over it. Return to the oven for a few minutes serve with roasted potatoes.

CARP STEW (Gedünsteter Karpfen)

2 lbs of carp	½ cup lemon juice
3 ozs onions = 1 large or	½ cup good stock
2 medium sized	3 ozs butter = 6 tablespoons
1 cup white wine	chopped parsley

Cut the onions and cook in a mixture of stock, white wine, salt and lemon juice. When done, put through a sieve. The cleaned fish is cut into slices convenient for serving, and simmered in this broth for about 20 minutes. Now take out, remove skin and the largest bones. Keep hot on a plate. The butter and the chopped parsley is now added to the sauce and poured over the fish.
This is usually served as an entrée, just with fresh toast.

FISH GULYAS (Fischgulyas)

2 lbs carp	1 cup sour cream
1 lb onions	2 tablespoons flour
paprika	2 cups stock

Slice and fry the onion till golden brown. Add the paprika, fry a little longer; now add the stock, cook for ten minutes with a lid on. Now add the fish; the liquid should just simmer, and leave on a small flame until fish is done. Add the cream, into which you have stirred the flour and serve with boiled potatoes.

PIKE WITH ANCHOVIES (Hecht mit Sardellen)

2 lbs pike	5 ozs butter = 2½ tablespoons
about 1 dozen anchovy slices.	

Wash, scale and clean the pike. Make slits along its back into which you insert the anchovy slices. Melt 1 oz butter in your baking dish, add the pike and bake until fish is done, basting all the time. Serve with hot anchovy sauce which is made the following way: crush two to three anchovies to a paste, melt the remaining 4 ozs of butter, mix with the paste and pour hot over the fish. Serve with parsley potatoes and a green salad.

PIKE WITH VEGETABLE SAUCE (Hecht mit Gemüse)

2 lbs pike (cut into slices) *2 carrots, 1 celery, 1 parsley root,*
1 lb veal bones *1 small onion*

Cut the vegetables into small pieces, fry the veal bones in 2 ozs fat, add the vegetables, and when fried on all sides, add three cups of water and salt, plus the juice of one lemon.

Cook for ten minutes, then on a low flame add the fish, simmer gently until this is done. Take fish out, strain soup, and put vegetables through a coarse sieve. Add some "Einbrenn" (2 tablespoons of flour fried light brown in 1 oz of butter), bring to the boil and simmer for a few minutes, then pour over fish which has been kept hot.

All these recipes can be made with any other similar sea fish of course, and might in this way prove to be useful additions to your present variety of methods.

Our mountain lakes and brooks yield wonderful trout, and some species which are in between a trout and a salmon. They are extremely delicious and are mainly prepared in a way which is common to most countries — fried in butter or cooked "Bleu" with hot butter. But let's continue with a few more unusual ways.

TROUT OVEN FRIED WITH MUSHROOMS & TOMATOES
(Gebratene Forelle mit Tomaten und Schwämmen)

2 trout (approx. 12 lbs each)   *5 medium sized mushrooms*
5 small tomatoes

Clean the fish and make incisions in the back, into which you insert the sliced mushrooms. Fry fish on both sides lightly, salt and pepper. Now put into a baking dish, in which you have melted some butter. Surround the fish with the rest of the sliced mushrooms and the sliced tomatoes. Pour a little more melted butter over it and the juice of one lemon. Bake in a hot oven for approximately 20 minutes, basting with butter and adding a little stock if it becomes necessary. Serve with parsley, potatoes and green salad.

FISH IN BÉCHAMEL

3 ozs butter = 6 tablespoons   *³/₄ pint cream = ³/₄ cup*
3 ozs flour = 1 cup   *2 lbs fish*

The fish is cut and stewed on its own in a little butter and lemon juice, also a few spoonfuls of stock. The Béchamel is then made in the usual way, and the fish served covered with this sauce.

FISH IN TOMATO SAUCE

The fish is prepared in the way described above and then put into a tomato sauce (see under Sauces). Serve with rice.

Now here is an unusual recipe for hot lobster:

PAPRIKALOBSTER AND NOODLES
(Paprikahummer mit Nudeln)

1 good sized lobster (or 2 tins)	1 cup white wine
5 ozs butter = ½ cup	1 tablespoon brandy
3 tablespoons paprika	salt, pepper

Béchamel

3 ozs butter = 6 tablespoons	¾ pint cream
3 ozs flour = 1 cup	

Make the Béchamel of the given quantities. Now in a different saucepan melt the 5 ozs butter, add the paprika and stir well over a low flame for 5 minutes. Now add the wine, the brandy and at last the Béchamel. Salt, pepper and simmer gently for a few minutes (if too thick for your liking add a little stock) then add the lobster which you have divided into smallish pieces, and leave just long enough for the lobster to get hot in the sauce, then serve with noodles. This is delicious and very quickly prepared if unexpected guests arrive!

FISH WITH PEPPERS AND TOMATOES
(Paprikafisch mit Tomaten)

2 lbs fish	6 large green peppers
3 ozs fat = 6 tablespoons	6 large tomatoes

Skin the tomatoes, seed and cut the peppers into strips. Put the fish into flour. Fry quickly on both sides until light brown and then remove from fat. In the same fat now fry the peppers a little, adding the quartered tomatoes, salt and pepper. Cover and simmer in its own juice until the peppers are soft. Now add the fish and simmer carefully until this is done.

Cold Fish Dishes (mainly used as Entrées)

CARP IN ASPIC (Karpfen in Aspik)

2 lbs carp
2 medium sized carrots
2 onions

bayleaves, peppercorns
lemon juice, thyme

Cut the vegetables into thin strips (Julienne) and cook them in seasoned water until they are done. Now strain the vegetables, put the liquid back into the saucepan, add the thyme, bayleaves and peppercorns and bring to the boil. The carp has meanwhile been cleaned and cut into portions. It is added to the stock, the flame is lowered and the fish is simmered very gently for about 15 minutes. Now lift out the pieces carefully and arrange them on an oblong dish (with a rim if possible) so that with the tail at one end and the head at the other, it gives the impression of a whole fish. Now garnish with the vegetables, and if you like, add pickled gherkins, also cut into strips and slices of hardboiled egg. The stock in which the fish has been cooked is now reduced by cooking it in an open saucepan. To each pint of liquid, add 1 tablespoon of gelatine, then clear the soup by straining it through a cloth, if necessary, by using the eggwhite method described in Beefsoup. Now spoon over the fish a little at a time, taking care not to disturb the vegetables, and when this is set, the rest is spooned on until the fish is covered as much as possible.

COLD PAPRIKA CARP (Kalter Paprikakarpfen)

2 lbs carp
2 lbs onions

2 pints water = 4 cups
3 teaspoons paprika

The carp is cleaned, washed and cut into slices. The onions are chopped and put into a saucepan with the water and the salt. When the onions are tender, add the paprika, stir and simmer a few minutes longer. Put this sauce through a sieve, return to saucepan and bring to the boil again, add carp, turn flame quite low and simmer fish in this for about 15 minutes. Lift fish out, arrange on dish and cover with the sauce, leave to set.

I   HERRINGSALAD (Heringsalat)

½ lb small potatoes

2 medium sized apples

2 pickled gherkins

4 pickled herrings (with soft roes)

½ pint sour cream = ½ cup

½ oz capers

salt, vinegar, ¼ pint oil

Take the soft roes out of the fish, put into basin and to this add the oil, gradually stirring as you would a mayonnaise. When all the oil is used up, add the sour cream, the chopped capers, salt, pepper and vinegar to taste. Into this marinade put the diced potatoes, the herrings which should be skinned, cleaned and cut into small slices, the peeled apples, also diced and the cucumbers cut finely. Mix carefully, and leave for about 3 hours before serving.

II

½ lb salad potatoes

2 apples

4 herrings (with soft roes)

1 tablespoon french mustard

2 medium sized cooked beetroot

   salt, pepper

½ lb cooked white beans

3 gherkins

¼ pint oil

1 tablespoon chopped onions

1 teaspoon chopped parsley

2 hardboiled eggs

Use the roes as in previous recipe, mix well with oil, the mustard vinegar, the very finely chopped onions and the parsley. Into this stir the beetroot (with all its juice) and the gherkins, which have all been put through the mincer. Mix well, now add the cooked strained beans, the diced potatoes, the diced apples and the herrings cut into small strips.

MARINATED FRIED FISH (Pikante Bratheringe)

This is generally used for herrings (fresh) but can be applied equally well to other varieties cut into convenient slices. It can also be used for leftover fried fish.

57

The herrings are cleaned, washed and filletted. The fillets are dipped into flour, to which has been previously added a little salt. Now put the fish into hot oil in frying pan, the skin side first, and fry briskly on both sides. Put into earthenware basin, and in between each layer of fish put plenty of onion rings. When all the fish has been fried and put into the basin, pour the following sauce over it: Half a pint of good wine vinegar, half a pint of water, a quarter pint of white wine, a sprig of thyme, salt, pepper and a bayleaf are simmered for about ten minutes after the mixture has boiled up once. When cooled it is poured over the fish. Cover and allow to stand for about two days. Serve with potato salad.

FISH IN MAYONNAISE

Prepare a mayonnaise (see under Sauces) and into this put any cooked fish, plucked into small pieces. This is also an excellent way to use up leftovers of boiled fish. Boiled sliced or diced potatoes, diced gherkins, tomatoes can be added. If served on a bed of fresh green salad makes an appetising meal, which can be prepared quickly.

For cooking any fish, we usually cook a few vegetable roots, a bayleaf, some peppercorns in salted water, to which a little vinegar has been added. The fish is simmered only in this broth, which should previously have boiled for about ten minutes.

FISH IN ASPIC

2 pints aspic	*6 gherkins*
½ lb fish (the cooked flesh of the fish only)	*6 hardboiled eggs*
	tomatoes

The aspic is warmed, and then left to cool slightly. A little is now poured into a mould (a deeper dish will do, or a ricering) approximately half an inch deep. The mould is then put in the icebox until the aspic jelly is set. Now put in the sliced hardboiled eggs and pieces of sliced and peeled tomato, then a little more of the aspic and return to icebox again until it is set.

Now fill in the fish mixed with the diced gherkins. Pour over the rest of the aspic and leave to set. When serving turn out on a bed of finely cut lettuce and serve with a mayonnaise.

All the recipes given for carp can be made with sea fish as well.

Essentials

I'm presuming that you are already a reasonably experienced cook, and that there is no need for me to go into details about things which are common to cooks all over the world. I'm sure you know all about cleaning your vegetables, washing your meat etc., so I'll just give you directions for things which are done differently here in Austria. But there are also a few things which I would like to repeat, although you may already be aware of them.

The peeling of:

Tomatoes: Just put them for a few seconds into boiling water, the skin comes off easily with a pointed knife.

Peaches: Are done the same way.

Apricots: Are done the same way.

Plums: Are done the same way.

Almonds: Are put into boiling water, brought to the boil once, left in the hot water for five minutes, then drained. The skin then comes off easily between your fingers.

Hazelnuts: Put the nuts on a baking sheet, then into the hot oven for about five minutes, the skin can be rubbed off between your hands. It is easier to do a few nuts at a time.

Chestnuts: Make a slit across the middle, put on a baking sheet in a hot oven for about five minutes, until shells and brown inner skins come off easily.

The cooking of:

Vegetables: They should be put into a little boiling water and cooked as little as possible, the water then used either for the vegetables or kept for soup or something similar. Green vegetables should be cooked uncovered as they keep their colour better that way.

Soups and Stews: Should never boil any more after they have boiled up once, just simmer slowly over a small flame.

Noodles, Spaghetti, Nockerl etc.: Should be cooked in plenty of boiling salted water. They really should be able to float in the saucepan. They must never be too soft, but should always be what the Italians call "Al dente" (so that you can still bite them without feeling they are soft as pulp). This should take about 15 to 20 minutes according to the size of the pasta. They should be rinsed under running cold water if they are not served straight away.

Rice: Should be put into a wire sieve and washed very thoroughly, even in lukewarm water if necessary, should then be left to dry completely on the sieve. It is then put into a saucepan with hot fat and fried well, until the ricecorns look glassy and transparent. Stir continually. Salt and water are added so that the water is about half an inch over the rice. Bring to the boil, then turn flame low and simmer quite slowly until rice is tender.

Butter: Should be used whenever possible, and not be substituted by margarine. This applies to all recipes where a piece of fresh butter is added before serving, and it certainly and definitely must be stressed for all crêmes in cakes. If you want to economise when baking, then try to use half and half. But you should a l w a y s spare that little suspicion of butter for greasing a baking tin or pudding basin. It makes a l l the difference I assure you.

Whisking eggwhite: It must not have a speck of the yolk in it, the bowl and the whisk must be spotless and completely dry. The tiniest spot of grease may spoil the sweet you are making. A pinch of salt helps to beat the eggs stiffly, but a pinch of sugar is equally good, for sweet dishes even better.

Sugar: Nearly all Austrian cake recipes call for icing sugar. You can use the finest caster sugar for baking, but use icing sugar for all crêmes.

Vanilla: Please try not to use vanilla essence when the recipes require vanilla. It is so easy to buy a vanilla pod and put it in a jar with a screw top. Fill the jar with icing sugar and you will always have vanilla-sugar handy. When vanilla flavouring in sauces is required, it is also a simple matter to cook a pod with the sauce. It is so much better than the essence.

Sour cream: Yoghourt or sour milk can be substituted if somebody is on a low fat diet. They both have to be whisked very well before use. Ordinary cream with a few drops of lemon juice mixed in thoroughly can also be taken if sour cream is unobtainable.

Flour: Should always be sifted before use.

Lemon rind: When it is used grated, it should always be the yellow outer skin of a fresh lemon which you have washed and dried before grating.

Horseradish: Should always be grated immediately before use.

Liver and Kidneys: Should only be salted after they are cooked, or they will harden.

Salt: A tiny pinch should be added to anything which is baked or steamed, to all cakes, it enhances the taste.
Should of course n o t be used in any crêmes, and n e v e r use salted butter.

Cakes: For testing to see if a cake is done, insert a metal knitting needle, and if it is sufficiently cooked, the needle will be quite clean when pulled out.

"Einbrenn": Is flour which has been roasted golden brown in fat, water or soup is added while stirring steadily, to avoid lumps, cold water must be used at first.

"Einmach": Is like an Einbrenn, used for thickening, only the flour must not take on any colour. If it calls for parsley, chopped mushrooms or finely chopped onions, this is done in the fat b e f o r e the flour is added. With Einbrenn they are added a f t e r the flour.

This brings us to:

Sauces

Most of these sauces are used in Austria when serving boiled beef. As this is eaten almost every day of the week, it is only natural that variations have been thought of. There are any number of sauces, cold and hot, but I have picked out just a few for your selection. In most restaurants you will find a dish: "Rindfleisch kalt und warm garniert" (Boiled beef with cold and warm garnishing) which is served on a special plate. In the middle is a large space for the meat, and this is surrounded by about nine smaller ones containing all the special sauces. (Try it when you are over here!) It is difficult to do this in one's own home as one usually never has so many garnishings prepared.

Not all these sauces are used for boiled beef only. Tomato sauce is served with Veal or with Pasta, Dill sauce can be served with braised Veal. I shall give you a note of the relevant fish or meat dish for each sauce.

Sauce Béchamel is white sauce, which is used as a basis for steamed puddings, some vegetables, soups, and most sauces with cheese that are used for baking — au gratin.

SAUCE BÉCHAMEL

To 1 oz of butter (2 tablespoons) take 1 oz (3 tablespoons) flour, on a small flame it should be stirred without the flour taking on any colour, add cold milk. This is the basis, it can be varied by adding grated cheese, nutmeg, according to the various recipes requiring it.

TOMATO SAUCE I (Paradeissauce I)

Cook the tomatoes — it is best to cut and stew them in their own juice without the addition of water. Put through a sieve. Make an Einmach of 3 ozs (6 tablespoons) of butter and 3 ozs (1½ cups) of flour, add ¼ pint (½ cup) of water, the tomato purée, salt and sugar to taste.

TOMATO SAUCE II (Paradeissauce II)

2 lbs tomatoes   salt, sugar
½ oz onions   1 small carrot, 1 small parsleyroot
1 oz fat (2 tablespoons)

Fry the chopped onion in the fat until golden brown, add the chopped carrot, the chopped parsley and lastly the flour. When golden brown, add a cup of stock or water (cold). To this add the tomatoes which are quartered and simmer until soft. Now put everything through a sieve, add sugar, salt and lemon juice to taste. Serve with boiled beef, roast or braised veal, or with any pasta.

TOMATO SAUCE NATUREL III (Paradeissauce III)

1 lb tomatoes   1 tablespoon oil
1 tablespoon white wine   salt, pepper, a pinch of sugar
1 tablespoon butter

Peel the tomatoes, take the seeds out after you have halved them, and sauté in the oil, which should be very hot, add the wine, butter and serve hot. This can be served with any meat.

DILL SAUCE (Dillensauce)

*3 dessertspoons finely chopped
dill
1/4 pint sour cream*

*1 cup clear beefbroth or stock
1 tablespoon butter
1 tablespoon flour, half a lemon*

Melt the butter and sauté 1 dessertspoon of the dill in this. Add the butter, taking care not to let it get brown. Pour the cold stock on this, stir well, bring to the boil and simmer slowly after you have added salt, the juice of half a lemon, a pinch of sugar. After five minutes, add the two dessertspoons of dill and the sour cream, simmer a little longer, but don't let it boil. Serve with beef or braised veal.

CAPER SAUCE (Kapernsauce)

*1 oz butter (2 tablespoons)
1 oz flour (3 tablespoons)
1/2 oz chopped onions*

*1 tablespoon chopped parsley
1 oz chopped capers*

Fry the onions golden in the fat, add the parsley and the flour (which should not get brown). Add two cups of stock, water or clear soup and the chopped capers. Do not add salt, as the capers are usually rather salty. A 1/4 pint of sour cream can be added if liked.

MUSHROOM SAUCE (Schwammerlsauce)

*1/2 lb mushrooms
1 tablespoon chopped onions
1 tablespoon chopped parsley*

*3 ozs butter (6 tablespoons)
1 oz flour (3 tablespoons)
1/2 cup sour cream*

Fry the chopped onions golden in half the butter. Add the parsley and the flour; when golden brown add stock or water and the sliced mushrooms, which you have sautéed in the rest of the butter. Just before serving, add the cream, simmer for a few moments, but do not boil.

If you don't need quite so much sauce, add the mushrooms to the fried onions and the parsley and just add a dusting of flour, either at this point or added to the sour cream.

For serving with boiled beef, escallopes of veal, but also tastes very good with dumplings only.

CUCUMBER SAUCE (Gurkensauce)

1 large fresh cucumber
1 oz fat (2 tablespoons)
1 oz flour (3 tablespoons)

1 tablespoon chopped dill
1 cup of sour cream

Peel the cucumber, take out the seeds and cut into slices. Melt the fat and add the flour, stirring well; add two cups of stock or water and the cucumber, salt, a pinch of sugar and a drop of lemon juice. Simmer for half an hour. Now add the chopped dill and the sour cream.

CUCUMBER SAUCE (With Pickled Cucumbers)

This is made in the same way, except that the lemon and salt are omitted, as the pickled cucumbers are usually sour and salty. Both are served with beef.

ONION SAUCE (Zwiebelsauce)

½ lb onions
1 tablespoon of sugar
2 ozs butter (4 tablespoons)

2 ozs flour (½ cup flour)
1 tablespoon vinegar

Cut the onions. Melt the butter in which you brown the sugar and add the onions. When these too are browned, add the flour, salt, and when this in turn is also brown, add approximately two cups of clear soup or water. Pepper and vinegar are now added. Bring to the boil, then simmer slowly for 10 minutes. Put through a sieve and serve hot with boiled beef.

HORSERADISH SAUCE WITH WHITE ROLL (Semmelkren)

½ cup cream
1 roll

1 tablespoon butter
2 tablespoons freshly grated
horseradish

Take the rind off as thinly as you can of a day old roll. Put into a saucepan and cover with stock. When it is soft put saucepan on a low flame, add a little more soup, and with an eggwhisk beat until roll is quite dissolved. Now add the butter, the grated horseradish, salt, pepper and the cream. The sauce should not boil any more. Serve at once.

MUSTARD SAUCE (Senfsauce)

Is made of half the quantity of onions as in the Onion Sauce, but without the sugar and the onions should not be quite as brown. Before serving, add two tablespoons of french mustard.

ALMOND HORSERADISH (Mandelkren)

2 tablespoons of horseradish
1 oz skinned almonds
1 oz butter (2 tablespoons)

1 oz flour (3 tablespoons)
1 teaspoon sugar
salt, pepper to taste

Make an "Einmach" of the butter and the flour, add 1 cup of cold milk, boil and simmer until thick, add salt, sugar, pepper and the grated horseradish, serve at once.
These last sauces are served with boiled beef only.

ANCHOVY SAUCE (Sardellensauce)

1 onion
5 anchovies
1 oz butter (2 tablespoons)

1 oz flour (3 tablespoons)
½ lemon

Fry the butter in the flour, add stock, soup or water, bring to the boil. Add the anchovies, the lemonjuice, a pinch of sugar and pepper. Simmer for ten minutes then put through the sieve. For boiled beef or any steamed fish.

COLD SAUCES (Mayonnaise)

The most important of course being Mayonnaise, although we cannot claim this as "ours", we use it quite a lot.

All the ingredients must have the same temperature, which should be that of a normal room. If you keep the oil and the eggs in your ice-box, take them out at least 2 hours before using them.

Naturally, there are many alternatives for this dressing, but I personally find the following one the best:

3 egg yolks	*½ teaspoon french*
1 cup oil	*mustard*
¼ lemonjuice	*vinegar to taste*

To the egg yolks add the oil, but only a tiny drop at a time stirring well with a fork meanwhile.

Take care that you really add the oil drop by drop, or it will never be right. Once you see that the mayonnaise starts to thicken, you can pour the oil in more freely. Add salt, a pinch of sugar to taste, a few drops of lemon, vinegar, pepper and mustard are optional. If you use a mixer, the whole thing becomes much easier of course, but there are some experienced cooks who maintain that it is really the "elbowgrease" that makes a good mayonnaise or crême. The "fluffiness" is, as you probably know, achieved by the air circulating while beating, and there is something in the fact that more air seems to be absorbed when it is done by hand. If you want to keep the mayonnaise for some time, add a tablespoon of boiling water to it when it is finished and mix well. If for some reason or other the mayonnaise does not mix properly, don't despair. Start a fresh one with just one yolk of egg, adding the oil carefully in drops only, and once this new mixture is thick, add one small teaspoon of the first one, stirring all the time, and this way add gradually the whole mixture to the new one.

ASPIC

I expect you are also able to buy ready made aspic as we do here but nevertheless, I shall give you an easy recipe for it, in case you'd like to try your hand at it. For the r e a l thing you need several kinds of bones, chopped beef, egg whites and so on, but most important of all, plenty of time and patience. But I have a simple method which I find just as good:

To 1 pint of stock (cleared beef, chicken or fish broth) — this must also be cleared of all fat, this is done when the soup is quite cold — add 1 ounce of gelatine. This can be either powdered or leaf gelatine, but must be dissolved in a little water first. Add a few drops of lemon to taste. Leave to set. It can then be poured into a glass jar and be kept in the ice for some time.

Aspic is used in many ways: 1. On a buffet supper or on open sandwiches it is advisable to brush them with melted aspic, it gives them a fresher look and prevents them from becoming dry so quickly. Heat the aspic until it is liquid, then stir until cool, it should be brushed on when it has reached the consistency of oil. 2. Alternatively, you can mix it with an equal part of mayonnaise, and then brush over your cold buffet. For this you heat the aspic, and then stir until cool, mix with an equal part of mayonnaise. For colour one can add finely minced spinach or tomato purée. 3. Aspic used for decoration: it looks very attractive when chopped, or diced, and can then be arranged around any cold dish. 4. For making cold moulds and salads. Line the mould with the aspic as follows: Fill the shape to the brim with liquid aspic. Put into ice-box, as soon as the outer layer is set, pour out the liquid aspic and put the form back into the ice and start the decorations. Eggs, gherkins or whatever you use, should be dipped into liquid aspic first and stuck to the sides of the mould, which should stand in a bowl of ice while you are doing this, then your salad or meat can be put in with the rest of the aspic.

MAYONNAISE SAUCES

Sauce Tartare: 1 teaspoon of chopped parsley, 1 teaspoon of chopped chives, 1 teaspoon chopped gherkins are mixed with ½ pint of mayonnaise. If too thick, thin with a little cold clear soup.

Pink Sauce (Tomatenmayonnaise): ½ pint mayonnaise is mixed with 2 tablespoons of tomato purée.

Green Sauce (Grüne Mayonnaise): The same as Sauce Tartare only 1 tablespoon of raw or parboiled finely minced spinach is added. These last two sauces taste very well with cold meat, eggs, poultry.
A very good mayonnaise sauce for hot or cold steamed fish is:

Sauce Valerie: ½ pint mayonnaise, 2 anchovies, 1 tablespoon of capers, 1 teaspoon of very finely grated onions. Chop the capers and the anchovies as finely as you can, mix with the onion to the mayonnaise.
Now an excellent Sauce Orange to go with hot or cold venison similar to Sauce Cumberland (the recipe for which I will give you after this one, in case you don't know it, although this actually comes from England, and is not Austrian).

69

Sauce Orange: 2 tablespoons of orange marmalade, 2 tablespoons of cranberry or redcurrant jelly, the juice of half a lemon, and half an orange, a few drops of Worcester sauce, 1 tablespoon of freshly grated horseradish. Mix all the ingredients, lastly adding the freshly grated horseradish. N.B. Make sure that the marmalade is not too chunky.

Sauce Cumberland: 3 tablespoons cranberry jelly, 2 tablespoons of madeira or red wine, pinch of english mustard powder. Mix the jelly with the wine, the mustard, the juice of half an orange and the finely grated rind of half an orange.

The following sauces are served with plain boiled beef:

Chive Sauce (Schnittlauch Sauce): Chopped chives are added to a mayonnaise which has been thinned to the consistency of thick cream with some cold clear soup.

Horseradish Sauces (Krensaucen):

With Vinegar. 4 tablespoons of grated horseradish are put into a bowl, ½ a cup of boiling clear soup is poured over this, then left to cool. Now mix with 1 tablespoon vinegar, 2 of oil, salt, pepper and sugar to taste.

With Apples. Prepare as above, when ready add one finely grated large apple.

With Cream. Mix 1 cup of thick cream with 1 tablespoon of good wine vinegar, 1 tablespoon of lemon juice, a little sugar and salt. To this add some freshly grated horseradish until you obtain a thick consistency. Alternatively, sour cream can be used.

Egg Sauce (Eier Sauce): Chop 4 hard boiled eggs. Add 1 teaspoon of chopped chives, 1 teaspoon of mustard, 2 tablespoons of oil, salt, pepper and a pinch of sugar, 1 teaspoon of vinegar, lemon juice to taste. Mix very well. If liked, the eggs can be put through a sieve before being mixed with the other ingredients.

Dumplings, Potatoes, Rice etc.

(Beilagen)

WHITE ROLL DUMPLINGS (Semmelknödel)

5 rolls
1 egg and one egg yolk
fat, flour, salt and pepper

chopped parsley
1 cup of milk

Cut the rolls (which should be at least a day old) or their equivalent in white bread, into tiny cubes. Roast them in about 1 oz of fat (bacon fat can be used). Mix the eggs with the milk and pour over dumplings and leave for half an hour. Add as much flour as the mixture will take to form good sized dumplings. Drop into boiling salted water and cook for about ten minutes. Dumplings are very good with all meat in sauces and especially so with Sauerkraut and boiled ham. For using up dumplings which are uneaten, see under "Leftovers".

TYROLEAN DUMPLINGS (Tirolerknödel)

The same as above, but add ½ lb of diced ham. These dumplings are usually cooked in soup, and in the Tyrol are served as a main dish together with the soup. In Vienna they are mainly served plain with a salad, preferably lettuce.

BACON DUMPLINGS (Speckknödel)

Are the same with bacon substituted for the ham.

MUSHROOM DUMPLINGS (Schwammerlknödel)

Add sautéed mushrooms to the mixture instead of bacon or ham.

DUMPLINGS COOKED IN A NAPKIN (Serviettenknödel)

4 rolls
2 eggs and one yolk
2 ozs butter (2 tablespoons)

a little butter and breadcrumbs for serving

Melt the butter, add the eggs and half a cup of milk, pour over the rolls which you have cut into cubes. When all the liquid has been absorbed, form a long roll which you place in a napkin (which has been previously wrung out in cold water). Fold over dumpling and tie the ends loosely and place into boiling salted water, cook for about half an hour. Take out, cut into slices, and serve sprinkled with breadcrumbs fried in butter. This Knödel is served with meat, but can also be served with stewed fruit as a dessert.

BREADCRUMB DUMPLINGS (Bröselknödel)

½ lb breadcrumbs (3 cups)
2 dessertspoons flour
2 eggs

2 tablespoons fat
salt, a little grated nutmeg
(optional)

Cream the fat well, add the salt, the nutmeg and stir in the eggs, now beat the flour and the breadcrumbs into the mixture. Leave covered for about 25 minutes. Form into small dumplings which should be cooked in boiling salt water.

SEMOLINA DUMPLINGS (Grießknödel)

2 ozs butter (2 tablespoons)
½ pint milk (½ cup)
4 ozs semolina (¾ cup)

2 eggs
2 rolls
1 oz butter (1 tablespoon)

Fry the cubed rolls in 1 oz butter. Bring the 2 ozs butter and the milk to the boil in a saucepan, add the semolina and on a small flame stir until a thick dumpling is formed. When cool, add the eggs, the fried breadcubes, salt. Leave for ten minutes and then make into medium sized dumplings which you cook in boiling salted water for about 10 minutes. Serve with Meat in sauces or as a dessert with Plum compôte.

SEMOLINA DUMPLINGS WITH FRIED BACON
(Speckgrießknödel)

Are a good meal in themselves. 2 ozs of fried bacon cut into small cubes or strips are added at the same time as the breadcubes. These dumplings are very tasty just served with a salad, preferably lettuce.

I   POTATO DUMPLINGS (Erdäpfelknödel)

½ lb potatoes
3 ozs semolina (½ cup or
   1 tablespoon)

1 egg yolk
½ oz butter (1 tablespoon)
2½ ozs flour (²/₃ cup)

Put the boiled potatoes through a sieve, add the semolina, the egg yolk, salt and the butter. Make into a dough. Form into dumplings and simmer slowly in salted water. Serve at once.

II   POTATO DUMPLINGS

1 lb potatoes
2 ozs butter (2 tablespoons)
3 rolls

1½ ozs flour (slightly more than
   ⅓ cup)
1 egg and 1 yolk
salt

Beat the butter well with the eggs, add the rolls which you have cut into cubes and fried in a little fat. Add the potatoes which you have cooked and put through a sieve, add the flour and the salt and cook in boiling salted water for 15 minutes.

CREAM CHEESE DUMPLINGS (Topfenknödel)

2 ozs butter (2 tablespoons)
½ lb cream cheese
3 ozs semolina (one cup or
  1 tablespoon)

milk
2 eggs
3 rolls

Soak the rolls in a litte milk and water, squeeze well and put through a sieve. Add to this the cream cheese, the eggs which you have beaten well with the butter, and lastly, add salt and the semolina. Leave under cover for about 1 hour.

Now mould into medium sized dumplings, and boil gently for 6 minutes in a wide saucepan with boiling salted water. Lift out carefully and put into breadcrumbs fried in butter. Can be served with meat or stewed fruit.

SMALL DUMPLINGS (Nockerl)

1 lb flour (2 cups)
3 ozs fat (6 tablespoons)
1 pint milk or milk and water
  (2 cups)

2 ozs fat for frying (4 tablespoons)
2 eggs

Beat the 3 ozs fat thoroughly, add the eggs, the flour and the liquid. You should have a large bowl and wooden spoon for this. Mix all ingredients and beat very well, giving this some time, as the mixture is only ready when the dough comes away easily from the wooden spoon. Place into boiling water (salted) on a small spoon which you dip into the boiling water first, so that the Nockerl slide off easily. (There are also sieves which in parts have fairly large holes, and the dough can be stirred into the water through these. Or you can try the quick Viennese method of putting one large blob of dough onto a wooden board (which should have a handle) and holding this over the saucepan with the boiling water with a large knife "shave" the nockerl off into the boiling water, stirring from time to time so that they don't stick together. Boil for ten minutes, take out, and rinse under cold running water. Now melt 2 ozs fat in a large saucepan, put the drained Nockerl into this, stir well, and serve hot. For using up uneaten Nockerl see under Leftovers.

Wassernockerl

Are cheap to make and also taste very good. You just use flour salt and water. To ½ pint of water add about ½ lb of flour and salt, beat well and continue as in above recipe. All noodles (spaghetti, maccaroni etc.), are cooked in boiling salted water, rinsed under the cold water tap and are warmed up again in a saucepan with a little melted fat.

RICE

When served with meat and not as a sweet, we usually like our rice so cooked that each rice-corn is separate. To achieve this the following rules are essential: the rice must be washed and dried thoroughly (dry it either in the oven or over a small flame in a saucepan, stirring all the time, or if there is enough time, let it dry on a sieve). Allow for 1 lb rice (2 cups) 3 ozs fat, and three cups of soup or water. Now there are two alternative methods for preparing it. 1. Fry the rice in the fat stirring well, add salt and the liquid, bring to the boil, then lower flame immediately and cover saucepan, then over the lowest flame possible, and an asbestos plate, let rice stand until soft. But don't stir! This will take ¾ hour. We usually put half an onion (some people stud this with a few cloves) to the rice, and remove this before serving. 2. Bring the liquid to the boil with the fat and the salt, add the rice. Bring to the boil again, cover and put into the hot oven. This way it is done in about 15—20 minutes.

TOMATO RICE (Paradeisreis)

2 tablespoons of tomato purée are added to the rice.

RISI-PISI

3 ozs of small green peas (tinned, frozen or fresh) are added to the rice. The best method is to add the cooked peas to the cooked rice.

MUSHROOM RICE (Schwammerlreis)

Sautéed mushrooms are added.

SEMOLINA NOODLES (Griessnudeln)

1 lb noodles
5 ozs semolina (1 cup)

¼ pint milk (¼ cup)
3 ozs fat (6 tablespoons)

Fry the semolina golden brown in the fat, cover with the milk, put a lid over and leave on a very low flame until all the liquid has evaporated. Now mix the noodles which you have cooked and rinsed with the semolina. Serve hot with meat and gravy, or as a sweet with stewed fruit.

BREADCRUMB NOODLES (Bröselnudeln)

Breadcrumbs are fried golden brown in a little fat and then mixed with cooked noodles or Fleckerln. Serve as above recipe.

CABBAGEPASTA (Krautfleckerln)

1 lb of Fleckerl or broken noodles
1 small head of white cabbage, or the remaining inner part of a cabbage the outer leaves

of which you might have used for Krautwürstel (see under Meat)
1 oz fat (1 tablespoon)
1 medium sized onion
salt, pepper, sugar

Cook the Fleckerl as described before. Now shred the cabbage finely and fry in the fat in which you have already fried the chopped onion with a pinch of sugar. When nicely brown, add the Fleckerl, pepper and salt. You can serve this with meat. We eat it as a light main dish.

PARSLEY POTATOES (Petersilerdäpfel)

Are potatoes cooked in their jackets, or new ones which are then just scraped. Use small ones if possible or cut into halves or quarters. They are added to some melted fat (preferably butter) in a saucepan, salt and chopped parsley is added, cover with a lid and the pan is shaken well. Serve with the parsley still fresh and green. Some people prefer the parsley fried in the fat before the potatoes are added. But this robs the parsley of its many vitamins, and in my opinion is also less attractive.

FRIED WHOLE POTATOES (Mitgebratene Kartoffel)

Boiled potatoes are fried on all sides with the roast.

CREAMED POTATOES (Erdäpfelpurée)

1 lb potatoes   ½ pint milk (½ cup)
1 oz butter (2 tablespoons)

Peel and quarter the potatoes, cook in salted water until soft. Drain and put through a sieve, mix with the butter and when thoroughly blended, mix with the milk which should be boiling hot. Serve at once topped with fried onionrings.

BOILED SLICED POTATOES FRIED (Erdäpfelschmarren)

1 lb potatoes   1 oz fat (1 tablespoon)

The cooked and peeled potatoes are sliced and fried in hot fat, in which you can first fry some chopped onions.

POTATO CROQUETTES (Erdäpfelkroquetten)

1 lb potatoes   salt, nutmeg
1 egg   1 teaspoon grated cheese (optional)
1 oz butter (1 tablespoon)   egg, breadcrumbs for coating
3 ozs flour (¾ cup)

Cook the potatoes, drain and put through a sieve. When cool, mix with the egg, the grated nutmeg, the cheese, the butter and flour. Make into small balls or rolls, put into egg and breadcrumbs then fry in deep hot fat (not too many at a time). These are best served with game.

Vegetables

(Gemüse)

I am a little hesitant about this chapter. I think we might call it the weak point of our cooking. You see, we still cook vegetables in the same way as our mothers and grandmothers! Very ruthlessly, as far as vitamins are concerned. Oh yes, we know all about them but somehow with our vegetables we seem to forget it, unless we do them in what we call the English way, that is, cooked in a little salt water, and served with butter. On the other hand, we eat lots of salad, even with things no-one else seems to. So maybe that makes up for it. Anyway, the recipes here show you the way I myself, and most modern housewives in Austria do them — I would say it's in between the old and the modern vitamin saving methods. Perhaps you would also like to know the other methods in use. The "English" one I've already told you about, the butter is usually put on in one or two fresh pieces. Then, there is what we call the French way, which means again, cooking the vegetables in very little salted water, but this time the butter is served separately, and is melted or slightly browned, or the vegetables are put into melted butter straight away and cooked in this. Then there is the Polish method, again just cooked in boiling salt water, but when served, topped with breadcrumbs which have been fried in butter. The reason for my picking out the French, English and Polish methods, is not because this is necessarily representative of the way vegetables are done in any of these countries, it is simply what we have made of them. So they have really become a part of Austrian cooking. But now let me tell you how it is done in general.

CARROTS (Karotten)

2 lbs carrots	1 teaspoon sugar
2 ozs butter (4 tablespoons)	1 teaspoon chopped parsley
1 oz flour (3 tablespoons)	salt

Clean the carrots, slice thinly or cut into narrow strips. Put into a saucepan in which you have melted the butter and simmer until almost soft. Now add the flour and just a little soup or water, the chopped parsley and a knob of fresh butter.

PEAS (Erbsen)

Shell the peas and treat exactly as carrots in the first recipe.

CARROTS AND GREEN PEAS (Karotten mit Erbsen)

Take half carrots and half small green peas. Start off in the same way as with the above recipe by doing the carrots first and adding the peas a little later as they are more quickly cooked.

KOHLRABI

Are done in the same way, if there are any young leaves on top use them as well, chop finely, mix with the parsley and add to the Kohlrabi when they are cooked.

Cauliflower and **Asparagus** can both be treated as above.

MIXED SPRING VEGETABLES (Frühlingsgemüse)

A mixture of carrots, peas, Kohlrabi, asparagus tips and chopped parsley. It is best to do all of these separately, as they each require a different cooking time.

MIXED VEGETABLES (Mischgemüse)

Are a mixture of equal parts of carrots, small sprigs of cauliflower, green peas, Kohlrabi, strips of root celery and sliced green runner beans.

79

COS LETTUCE (Kochsalat)

5 heads of Cos lettuce
2 ozs butter (2 tablespoons)

1½ ozs flour (4½ tablespoons)
2 tablespoons chopped onions

Take off the coarse outer leaves of the lettuce, you can usually only make use of these if you take out the middle rib. Put all the leaves into a basin and pour some boiling water over them. Take the lettuce out, letting the water drip off, and chop very finely. It can also be put through the mincer. Fry onion golden, add the flour and the chopped lettuce, add a little water if necessary, salt and sugar to taste.

COS LETTUCE AND GREEN PEAS (Kochsalat mit Erbsen)

Are done the same way as the above recipe, and 1 lb of green peas are added.

4 w a y s f o r :

I   GREEN BEANS (Fisolen)

2 lbs beans
2 ozs flour (½ cup)
2 ozs butter (4 tablespoons)

1 oz onion
1 teaspoon vinegar
salt and pepper

String the beans and cut either into diagonal strips or straight across. Fry the chopped onions in the fat, add the flour and the parsley. Now add the beans which you have cooked in a little boiling water. Add as much of this water (about 1½ cups) as needed, plus one tablespoon of vinegar.

II   GREEN BEANS

Leave out the onion and the parsley and prepare as before. Add 1 oz of finely chopped dill when beans are almost done and right at the end, one cup of sour cream.

III   GREEN BEANS

Leave out the dill and add ½ teaspoon of mild paprika and a pinch of sugar to the sour cream.

In a little water and 3 ozs (6 tablespoons) of butter, 1 lb of cut beans are simmered until soft. Now sprinkle 1 oz (3 tablespoons) of flour over, stirring carefully, add a little soup, salt, pepper, vinegar to taste. Carrots, peas, cauliflower and shredded root of celery can also be prepared in this way.

5 w a y s f o r :

SAUERKRAUT

Much can be said in favour of Sauerkraut. I believe it saved many ship
crews from scurvy in olden times,
and is supposed to have many special vitamins. But I don't know
what happens to them if treated
the Viennese way, which is to
reheat several times! But it definitely
gains flavour and it is more than useful to have a dish which tastes even
better as a leftover. If it is too sour,

rinse the Kraut with cold water before preparing. Any fat can be used, but the best flavour is obtained when you use fat which you have yourself rendered down from bacon.

I   **SAUERKRAUT**

2 lbs Sauerkraut	*1 oz onion*
2 ozs fat (4 tablespoons)	*salt*

Stew the Sauerkraut in a little water, add the onion which should be first chopped and fried in the fat. Salt and simmer until tender.

II   **SAUERKRAUT**

2 lbs Sauerkraut	*1 oz onion*
2 ozs fat (4 tablespoons)	*2 potatoes*
2 ozs flour (½ cup)	*salt*

Put the Sauerkraut into a basin and cover with cold water. Fry the onion (till golden) add the flour. Strain the Sauerkraut and the water should now be added to the onions and flour. Stir well to avoid lumps forming. Now add the Sauerkraut and the two peeled potatoes which should be grated. Add some carraway seeds and simmer for 10 minutes.

III   SAUERKRAUT

2 lbs Sauerkraut   *2 ozs flour (½ cup)*
2 ozs bacon fat (4 tablespoons)   *1 to 2 cups soup*

Fry the bacon and leave in the small greaves. Add the flour and then the Sauerkraut, together with the soup. Stir well, and simmer for 10 minutes.

IV   SAUERKRAUT

1 lb Sauerkraut   *1 oz sugar (2 tablespoons)*
2 ozs butter (4 tablespoons)   *1 cup white wine*

Melt the butter and brown the sugar in it. Add the Sauerkraut, cover saucepan and simmer until almost done. Now add the white wine and simmer for a few more minutes.

V   SAUERKRAUT

2 lbs Sauerkraut   *1½ ozs flour (⅓ cup)*
2 ozs onion   *1 cup sour cream*
2 ozs sugar (4 tablespoons)   *½ tablespoon of fat (for frying*
3 ozs bacon fat (6 tablespoons)   *1 teaspoon paprika)*

Fry the onion in the bacon fat, add the sugar and when everything is golden brown, add the flour. Stir well and add the Sauerkraut, one cup of water or clear soup. When the Sauerkraut is done, fry the paprika in the fat in a separate pan, add to the Sauerkraut and just before serving, add the sour cream and simmer for a few moments.

WHITE CABBAGE WITH TOMATOES AND GREEN PEPPERS (Kraut mit Paprika und Paradeisern)

This is done in the same way as the white cabbage only three peeled tomatoes and three sliced green peppers are fried in the onions before the cabbage is added. If liked, a cup of sour cream can be added before serving.

SAVOY CABBAGE (Kohl)

2 lbs savoy cabbage
4 ozs fat (½ cup)
2 ozs flour (½ cup)

3 potatoes
1 clove garlic
salt and pepper

Wash the cabbage and take out the coarsest ribs. Shred finely and put into very little boiling salted water. Fry the flour light brown in the fat, add 1 cup of stock, add the cabbage which should be parboiled. Crush the garlic on a wooden board with salt and pepper with the blade of a knife. Add this to cabbage and grate the potatoes into it. Simmer until the cabbage has become a mash.

WHITE CABBAGE (Kraut)

2 heads cabbage
2½ ozs fat (5 tablespoons)
2 tablespoons flour

1 oz onion
2 tablespoons vinegar
carraway seeds

Shred the cabbage finely. Fry the onion in the fat, and when golden brown add the cabbage, the carraway seeds, salt and 2 tablespoons vinegar. Cover saucepan and simmer cabbage in its own juice on a very low flame. When done, add a little water or soup into which you have stirred the flour. Mix well and simmer for a few more minutes.

RED CABBAGE (Rotkohl)

2 heads red cabbage
2 ozs fat (½ cup)
1 medium onion
1½ ozs sugar (3 tablespoons)

1 medium apple
¼ pint red wine (¼ cup)
2 tablespoons flour
1 tablespoon vinegar

Fry the onions in the fat, add the sugar and fry all this golden

brown. Now add the shredded cabbage, the peeled and sliced apple and simmer with 2 cups of stock. As soon as the cabbage is done, dust with the flour (r e a l l y dust — stirring all the time to avoid lumps, even tiny ones forming). Add the vinegar and the wine and simmer for a few more minutes.

BLUE CABBAGE AND CHESTNUTS (Blaukohl mit Kastanien)

4 heads of cabbage (about 2 lbs)   *1½ ozs flour (4½ tablespoons)*
2 ozs fat (4 tablespoons)   *1 small onion*
5 to 6 peeled chestnuts   *1 teaspoon chopped parsley*
1½ ozs sugar (3 tablespoons)   *2 cups water*

Divide the cabbage into separate leaves and take out the coarse ribs. Put into boiling salted water. Strain, rinse in cold water and put into a sieve so that all the water can drip off, chop finely. Roast the flour lightly in the fat (it should not be brown) add the chopped onion and parsley, the stock, and the cooked and mashed chestnuts. Now add the chopped cabbage. For decoration, whole chestnuts can be used. They should be cooked first and then fried in a knob of butter to which you have added 2 teaspoons of icing sugar.

SPINACH (Spinat)

Wash the spinach and without adding water, put into a saucepan on a very low flame, together with a pinch of salt. When parboiled, put through a sieve, keeping all the liquid. Meanwhile, make an "Einmach" (see under Essentials) add the liquid of the spinach, beat well over a low flame, so that no lumps are formed, and now add the sieved spinach. Simmer slowly, add a piece of fresh butter. If you like the flavour you can either grate a little nutmeg into it, or half a clove of garlic, which must be mixed with salt on a board with the help of a knife. In this way, hardly any vitamins are lost as they are contained in the water, and one aims to cook the spinach as little as possible. But you can improve on that even, by putting the raw, washed spinach through the mincing machine and (if you like it very fine) after that through a sieve and add it like that to the Einmach. Again be careful that none of the liquid is lost.

3 ways for:

I MARROW (Kürbis)

1 marrow (3 to 4 lbs)
3 ozs fat (6 tablespoons)
2½ ozs flour (¾ cup)

1 tablespoon vinegar
1 cup cream
salt and ½ teaspoon paprika

Peel the marrow, cut into four sections, take out the seeds, shred finely, put into a basin, salt and leave for ½ an hour under cover. Now put into saucepan, together with all the liquid which has formed, but without any water. Simmer gently under cover. When done, add the flour which you have fried very lightly in the fat, the vinegar, cream and paprika and simmer for another five minutes.

II MARROW

1 marrow (3 to 4 lbs)
2 - 3 green peppers
2 - 3 medium tomatoes

2 ozs fat (4 tablespoons)
2 ozs flour (½ cup)

Peel the tomatoes and then slice (the skin comes off easily if you immerse them in boiling water for a few seconds). The green paprika are cut into strips. Now fry the paprika in the fat, but only a little, then add the tomatoes and the finely shredded marrow. There should be enough liquid of the vegetables that they can be simmered without the addition of water. When the marrow is done, add the cream into which you have stirred the flour.

III MARROW

Shred the marrow as before, put into tomato sauce (see under Sauces) and simmer until soft.

3 ways for:

I   LETSCHO

This is really a Rumanian dish which we have adopted, but it is a delicious way of preparing several vegetables.

2 - 3 onions	*6 - 7 tomatoes*
5 - 6 green paprika	*2 ozs fat (4 tablespoons)*

Cut the onions into rings, fry golden in the fat, add the green peppers cut into strips, lastly the peeled tomatoes. Simmer until soft. This can be served as vegetable only or as a main dish with Frankfurters or similar sausages cut into it and some rice.

II   LETSCHO

Prepare the same way as above, only 6 scrambled eggs are poured over the mixture when this is done. Then cook for a few minutes until eggs are set.

III   LETSCHO

This time omit the tomatoes and prepare only with onions, green peppers and the eggs.

3 ways for:

I   LENTILS (Linsen)

1 lb lentils	*1 teaspoon chopped parsley*
2 ozs fat (4 tablespoons)	*1 bayleaf*
2 ozs flour (½ cup)	*1 sprig of thyme*
1 oz onion	*1 teaspoon vinegar*
grated lemon peel	*1 teaspoon lemon juice*

Soak the lentils overnight in cold water, then cook in salted water with a sprig of thyme and bayleaf. When lentils are soft, stir in the flour which you have fried brown in the fat. Add the lemon juice and vinegar.

II   LENTILS

Are prepared in the same way, only the lentils are put through a sieve before the flour and fat are added.

III   **LENTILS**

2 lbs lentils	*1 pinch grated nutmeg*
2 pints clear beef broth	*1 oz butter (1 tablespoon)*

Cook the lentils in the beef broth and but through a sieve when they are soft. Bring to the boil again in the beef broth, add the nutmeg, simmer for a few minutes and serve with the fresh butter on top. This prevents a skin forming.

YELLOW DRIED SPLIT PEAS (Gelbe Spalterbsen)

1 oz butter (2 tablespoons)	*½ oz chopped onion*
1 lb peas	*½ teaspoon chopped parsley*

Cook the peas until soft, put through a sieve, stir in the butter and the chopped parsley before serving; top with fried onions.

Did you know that quite a number of vegetables taste excellently prepared like a Wiener Schnitzel? They are served as an entrée with a Sauce tartare (see under Sauces). They can also be served as a light main dish with a salad. The vegetables which taste best prepared like this are:

CAULIFLOWER (Karfiol)

Divide into several not-too-small sprigs, only the top part being used. The main stalk can be used for soup. The sprigs are parboiled slightly in salt water. Drain and when cool dip in flour, egg and breadcrumbs and fry.

ROOT OF CELERY (Zeller)

Is cut into thick slices which are parboiled first. Continue as in previous recipe.

MUSHROOMS (Pilze)

Only the heads are used (leave the stalks for soup). Don't parboil first.
The next two are mainly used as an accompaniment to meat.

APPLES (Äpfel)

Prepared in this way are excellent with roast pork (they are also good topped with some redcurrant jam and served as a sweet.

ONION-RINGS (Zwiebelringe)

Are served with roastbeef.

CUCUMBERS (Frische Gurken)

2 lbs cucumbers   *1 oz chopped dill*
1 oz butter (1 tablespoon)   *1 cup sour cream*

Cut off both ends of the cucumber, peel, cut into half and take out the seeds. Now cut into slices, sauté in the butter until soft without adding any liquid. Now add the chopped dill and the sour cream which you have mixed with the flour. Simmer for a few more minutes.

CELERY DUMPLINGS (Zellerknödel)

The root of the celery is peeled and shredded finely. Now add $1/8$ of the quantity of celery in the shape of a shredded onion, salt and pepper and add as much flour as is needed to form small dumplings. Fry in hot fat.
This brings us to another way in which vegetables can be used as a separate dish or as an entrée.

MUSHROOMS AND EGGS (Schwammerl mit Ei)

2 lbs mushrooms
3 ozs butter (6 tablespoons)
1 tablespoon chopped parsley
6 eggs

Sauté the sliced mushrooms in the butter until tender, add the parsley and the eggs which you have beaten well. Pour over mushrooms and leave on small flame till eggs are set.

GREEN PEAS AND HAM (Erbsen mit Schinken)

1½ lbs shelled green peas
2 teaspoons chopped parsley
3 ozs butter (6 tablespoons)
5 ozs cooked ham
2 ozs flour (½ cup)

Cook the peas in a little boiling salted water. Strain, keeping the liquid. Melt the butter, add the flour and the water in which you have cooked the peas, add a pinch of sugar, the parsley, the green peas and lastly the ham, which should be cut into small strips.

CAULIFLOWER AND HAM (Karfiol mit Schinken)

2 beads of cauliflower
(approx. 1½—2 lbs)
½ lb lean cooked ham
2 egg yolks
½ cup sour cream
1 oz grated cheese (3 tablespoons)
1 oz butter (1 tablespoon)
a little butter for the casserole
½ oz breadcrumbs (1½ table-spoons)

The cauliflower is cooked and parted into small sprigs. (Again only the top part is used — the coarse end can be used for soup.) Cut the ham into tiny cubes, butter a fireproof dish and sprinkle with breadcrumbs. Put in a layer of cauliflower, a layer of ham, a layer of

89

cauliflower and so on alternately. Mix the cream with the yolks, add the grated cheese and pour over the cauliflower. Sprinkle with breadcrumbs, put a few flakes of butter on top and bake for ½ an hour in a medium hot oven.

STUFFED TOMATOES (Gefüllte Paradeiser)

Take one or two tomatoes per person, preferably large ones. Cut off the stalk end. Take out the inside flesh and seeds (this is best done with a sharp pointed knife and a teaspoon, taking care not to spoil the shape of the tomato). The inside can be used as soup or for tomato sauce. Into the tomato shells you now put a drop of olive oil, salt and pepper, and place in a hot oven for about 5 minutes.

Now take out and fill with any of the various stuffings given below. The part which you have cut off previously can be put on as a "lid", or a few flakes of butter and some breadcrumbs are put on the filling. The tomatoes now go back into a fairly hot oven again for 10 minutes. This is also a good way to use up any leftovers for filling. For cold stuffed tomatoes, see under Cold Entrées.

VARIOUS FILLINGS

Cooked rice with chopped ham.

Cooked rice with mushrooms.

Ragout of chicken (the meat is cut into small pieces and a little gravy and rice are added).

Stewed mushrooms.

Any vegetables made the Viennese way.

A little gulyas with the meat cut quite small and very little gravy.

Brains and Eggs.

Mushrooms and Eggs.

Mashed or creamed potatoes into which you have grated some cheese.

Any of these other vegetables can also be filled and cooked this way:

1. Large Mushrooms.
2. Large pieces of fresh cucumber.
3. Large potatoes.
4. Root of Celery.
5. Kohlrabi.

(The last three should be cooked first before they are filled.)

BEAN RISSOLES (Bohnenschnitzel)

1 lb beans	*½ tablespoon chopped parsley*
1 egg	*½ lb diced ham or sausage*
1 oz onion	*2 ozs breadcrumbs (6 tablespoons)*

Soak the beans overnight and cook until soft. Put through a sieve. Add the egg, the chopped fried onions, chopped parsley, salt and the diced ham. Now dip into flour, egg and breadcrumbs and fry in hot fat. Serve with salad.

N o t e : You can of course use the same quantity of beans from a tin.

STEAMED SPINACH PUDDING (Spinatpudding)

3 ozs butter (6 tablespoons)	*1 teaspoon chopped parsley*
6 eggs	*2 white rolls*
1 lb raw spinach (6 ozs cooked spinach)	*1 oz breadcrumbs (3 tablespoons)*
	½ cup sour cream

Beat the butter well, then add one yolk at a time, always stirring well. Add the cooked spinach which you have put through a sieve, or chopped very finely, and the chopped parsley. Add the rolls and the cream (the rolls having first been soaked in a little milk and

91

water, pressed out and put through the mincer). Mix very well. Now beat the six whites of egg into which you fold the breadcrumbs. Butter a pudding form, sprinkle with breadcrumbs. Mix the two parts of the pudding carefully and put into the form. Now place into boiling water after you have covered the form with a lid. Cover saucepan and cook for about one hour. Should be served sprinkled with breadcrumbs which you have fried in butter, and can be surrounded by a ring of chopped ham (approximately ¼ lb).

VEGETABLE PUDDING (Gemüsepudding)

3 ozs sliced mushrooms	2 ozs butter (4 tablespoons)
3 ozs sliced green beans	5 eggs
3 ozs green peas	¼ pint milk (¼ cup)
3 ozs cauliflower	¼ lb flour (1 cup)
1 oz grated cheese (1 tablespoon)	2 ozs butter (4 tablespoons)

First make the Béchamel (see under Essentials). Leave to cool. Now beat the 2 ozs butter well, add the five yolks (one at a time). Add to the Béchamel. The vegetables should all be parboiled separately, then drained of all liquid and added to the Béchamel mixture. Beat the five whites of eggs stiffly, mix with the rest, and put in a buttered and floured pudding basin. Cover, cook for an hour in boiling water, serve with grated cheese.

I   VEGETABLE RISSOLES (Gemüseschnitzel)

4 rolls	1 egg
1 cup milk	6 ozs butter (¾ cup)
4 ozs spinach	1 oz mushroom
½ tablespoon chopped onion	½ tablespoon chopped parsley

Take the rind of the rolls, soak in milk, squeeze out and put through a sieve. Now mix the chopped and fried onion with the parsley, the spinach which should be chopped raw, salt and pepper and the egg. Sauté the sliced mushrooms and add to the mixture. If too soft, add a few breadcrumbs. Form into rissoles, dip into flour, egg and breadcrumbs and fry.

II   VEGETABLE RISSOLES

3 ozs carrots	*1 egg*
3 ozs root celery	*2 ozs grated cheese (6 tablespoons)*
3 ozs cauliflower	*1 lb boiled potatoes*
3 ozs mushrooms	*salt, pepper and nutmeg*
1 medium onion	

Peel the potatoes, cook until soft, put through a sieve. When cool, mix with the egg, the grated cheese, salt, pepper and nutmeg.

Now add the sliced mushrooms which you have sautéd a little in the chopped and fried onion. Add the vegetables which have been diced and cooked. Make into rissoles and dip in breadcrumbs. Fry, and serve with hot tomato sauce.

III   VEGETABLE RISSOLES

½ lb mixed vegetables (carrots,	*1 ½ pints milk*
peas, cauliflower)	*1 oz butter (2 tablespoons)*
5 ozs oats	*1 egg*

Cook the oats slowly in the milk until they are soft and thick. Leave to cool slightly, add the butter, the egg and the boiled and diced vegetables. Leave for an hour and form into rissoles and fry. If the mixture should be too soft, add a few breadcrumbs. All these vegetable rissoles can be improved by adding a little chopped ham.

MUSHROOM RISSOLES (Pilzschnitzel)

1 lb mushrooms	*Béchamel*
1 oz chopped onion	*2 ozs butter (4 tablespoons)*
1 teaspoon chopped parsley	*½ cup milk*
3 ozs butter (6 tablespoons)	*3 ozs flour (¾ cup)*
	2 eggs

Chop the onion and the parsley, sauté in a little butter, add the sliced mushrooms. Prepare the Béchamel (see under Essentials) stir in the eggs and the mushrooms and onions. When cool, form into rissoles (again, if the mixture is too soft add a few breadcrumbs) and fry.

Salads

Form a very important part of the Austrian menu. In other countries, the salad is more an entrée or is eaten between courses. Elsewhere, salads are only served with cold cuts etc. We serve salads with almost anything, sometimes even with meat which is well covered with gravy, but this is a matter of taste of course. We also still maintain a difference between winter and summer salads, although nowadays, most vegetables can be obtained from the deep freeze, I think it is still rather nice to ring the changes with the seasons, so I'll divide this chapter also into summer and winter salads.

The most basic dressing used here is of course oil, vinegar, salt and a little sugar. I don't know if I should give you exact quantities — it is so much a matter of taste, you are a lover of oil perhaps, or maybe you prefer lemon instead of vinegar, more or less sugar and so on. The vinegar should always be a good quality, preferably winevinegar. I shall give you my own household recipe for salad, as it always seems to be well received by family and visitors alike.

Winter Salads

I'm starting with lettuce, as this is really eaten all the year round, and when served with bacon is only eaten during the colder part of the year.

HEADS OF LETTUCE (Grüner Salat)

2 firm heads	*¼ cup of vinegar*
½ cup of good salad oil (olive oil is seldom used)	*½ teaspoon salt*
	a small teaspoon of sugar

Wash and trim lettuce, shake dry or leave to drip on a sieve. Just before serving add the salt, sugar, oil and lastly, the vinegar. This is the basis, you can now add to this: serve with quartered eggs on top, serve mixed with chives and or parsley, add a spoonful of French mustard to the oil, mix a little chopped dill with the vinegar.

HEADS OF LETTUCE WITH BACON (Mit Speck)

2 heads of lettuce
2 ozs fat bacon

salt, sugar as before
½ cup vinegar

Wash and trim lettuce as previously, put on sieve. Now fry the bacon which you have cut into small cubes until these are golden brown, take out and keep hot. Let the fat cool (but not so much that it sets) and pour over the lettuce which you have already mixed with the vinegar, salt and sugar (the only instance where the vinegar comes first!). Before serving, sprinkle with baconcubes.

Chicory can be prepared in the same way.

WHITE CABBAGE SALAD (Krautsalat)

1 head of cabbage
allow 2 parts of oil to 1½ parts of
vinegar according to taste and
size of the cabbage

1 teaspoon french mustard
  (optional)
pepper, salt, a little sugar
1 teaspoon carraway seeds

Remove the stalks from the cabbage, shred finely, put into a large basin and cover with boiling salted water, and leave for an hour. Drain off water, and squeeze the cabbage lightly between both hands. Mix the ingredients for the dressing in a bowl and toss the salad into it.

Red cabbage can also be prepared in this way.

WARM CABBAGE SALAD (Warmer Krautsalat)

Proceed the same way as in previous recipe, but while the cabbage remains covered, prepared the dressing from half a cup of good vinegar, with half a cup of water, a teaspoon of carraway seeds, sugar, salt (take care that you don't add too much as there is already some in the soaking water). When you have drained the cabbage as in the previous recipe, bring the dressing to the boil and pour over cabbage; leave for 10 minutes. Now drain, but retain all the liquid, which you boil up again and pour over. Do this as often as there is any liquid left. Before serving, pour 2 ozs of fried bacon fat (w i t h the little greaves that remain from frying) over the salad.

I   BEETROOT SALAD (Rote Rübensalat)

3 lbs cooked beetroot (about 6)	*salt*
3 ozs horseradish	*1 tablespoon carraway seeds*
1 pint vinegar	*½ oz sugar (1 tablespoon)*

Grate the beetroot or put through the mincer with the freshly grated horseradish (if it brings tears to your eyes while grating remind yourself that it is healthy!). Put into a jar and cover with the vinegar which you have mixed with the sugar, salt and carraway seeds. A few grated apples (one or two medium sized) taste good mixed with the beetroot. Drain off any superfluous liquid before serving.

II   BEETROOT SALAD

This salad can be prepared in advance, so you can prepare a larger quantity and keep it in a covered glass.
The same ingredients as before. Slice the beetroot and the horseradish, put in layers in a jug and cover with the vinegar which you have boiled with the sugar, salt and carraway seeds. This salad should stand at least two days before serving.

LENTIL SALAD (Linsensalat)

1 lb lentils	*¼ pint vinegar (½ cup)*
¼ pint oil (¼ cup)	

Cook the lentils until tender (but not too much). Strain, and while still warm pour the dressing over. This should be prepared about two hours before serving. Some people like a spoonful of french mustard in their dressing and some add very finely chopped onions mixed into the lentils.

BEAN SALAD (Bohnensalat)

Prepare exactly the same as above, only substitute beans for the lentils, but this time a medium sized onion cut up finely is a m u s t!

CELERY SALAD (Zellersalat)

4 celery roots (about 1½ lbs)	*1 - 2 tablespoons vinegar*
lemon juice (equivalent to two	*1 teaspoon sugar*
lemons)	*¼ pint oil (¼ cup)*

Wash and peel roots, cut into two halves, cook in salted water until soft — if you put a few drops of the lemon juice into the cooking water, it will remain whiter. Leave to cool and cut into slices as thinly as possible. Now cover with the oil, sugar, salt and remaining lemon juice, and leave to stand. If necessary, add the spoon of vinegar. Don't mix too much as the celery breaks easily.

RADISH SALAD (Rettichsalat)

Red radishes are cut finely and are mixed with oil, vinegar, salt and a little sugar. If the large black or white radishes are used, it is better to slice them finely, salt them and keep them covered for an hour. They are then squeezed dry of all salt water, marinated with vinegar, oil, sugar, but without salt. This treatment makes them more tender.

SALAD OF FRESH SAUERKRAUT (Sauerkrautsalat)

Sauerkraut is rinsed in cold water, drained, chopped and mixed with oil, a pinch of sugar. Salt and vinegar are usually not necessary, carraway seeds are optional.

POTATO SALAD (Erdäpfelsalat)

2 lbs potatoes (a waxy and small variety is best)
4 tablespoons oil
2 tablespoons vinegar

salt, pepper, a pinch of sugar
1 medium sized onion chopped very finely

The potatoes are cooked in their jackets, and while still slightly warm are sliced into a bowl in which you have already mixed the other ingredients. Leave for an hour after you have mixed carefully. If preferred, the onions can be left out and chopped parsley may be added.

ROOT CELERY AND POTATO SALAD
(Zeller- und Erdäpfelsalat)

Celery is cooked in the way described and mixed half and half with a potato salad.

POTATO SALAD AND ENDIVES (Mit Endiviensalat)

Into a finished potato salad, finely cut Endives are added and mixed just before serving.

MAYONNAISE SALAD

Is potato salad without onions mixed with a mayonnaise. If necessary a little more vinegar can be added.

VEGETABLE SALAD WITH MAYONNAISE
(Gemüsesalat mit Mayonnaise)

In Austria this is called "Gemüsemayonnaise" and consists of a mayonnaise in which are equal parts of tiny diced potatoes, carrots, root celery and green peas, all cooked of course. It should be as thick as a potato salad.

Any of the following cooked vegetables can be used as a salad with an oil, vinegar or lemon dressing, salt, pepper and a pinch of sugar.

Sliced mushrooms, parboiled in a little water.

Sprigs of Cauliflower, parboiled in a little water.

Leeks, parboiled in a little water.

Asparagus, parboiled in a little water.

Green peas, parboiled in a little water.

They can all be served in a mayonnaise as well.

Sometimes a mixed salad (gemischter Salat) is served, especially in Restaurants, and in winter will consist of: beetroot salad, a few lettuce leaves, bean salad, cabbage salad, potato salad. They are served in one dish, a small portion of each next to the other. In the summer, a mixed salad consists of lettuce, tomato salad, cucumber salad, green pepper or green bean salad.

Summer Salads

TOMATO SALAD (Paradeissalat)

Tomatoes are peeled (see Essentials) sliced and put into a dressing consisting of oil (2 tablespoons), vinegar (1 tablespoon), salt, pepper, a pinch of sugar, chopped parsley. Mix all ingredients well and arrange the tomatoes carefully in this. Chopped onions can also be added.

GREEN PEPPER SALAD (Paprikasalat)

Green peppers are washed, the seeds are taken out, and are then cut into thin strips. Put into a basin and cover with boiling salted water. Cover and leave for an hour. Drain and mix with oil, chopped onions, pepper, salt, a pinch of sugar, vinegar.

TOMATO AND GREEN PEPPER SALAD

Prepare the tomato salad as above, add chopped onions and finely cut green peppers.

CUCUMBER SALAD (Gurkensalat)

Cut off the ends of the cucumbers (they are usually bitter). Now peel and slice finely. In Austria a slicer called a "Hobel" is used for cutting it very thinly. In older Austrian cookery books you will find that they advise you to cut the cucumbers, salt, leave to stand and then squeeze out all the liquid. This is considered quite wrong from a medical viewpoint (although it makes no difference to the taste) as you then get all the cellulosis of the cucumbers, of which they mostly consist, without their liquid, which alone makes it easily digestible. Well, we've got as far as slicing the cucumbers, now add to about 2 lbs of cucumbers ⅛ pint of oil, ⅛ pint of vinegar, salt, pepper, a pinch of sugar, a tablespoon of french mustard. Sprinkle with red paprika.

Alternatively: leave out the paprika and mix with chopped chives, or: if liked, rub the saladbowl with a clove of garlic and add finely chopped onions to the salad.

II   CUCUMBER SALAD

Peel and slice the cucumbers as before, cover with sour cream and salt, if not sour enough add a dash of lemon juice. It can either be sprinkled with paprika or chopped chives or mixed with plenty of chopped dill.

GREEN BEAN SALAD (Fisolensalat)

Young tender runner beans are cleaned and sliced, cooked in a little salt water, but not too tender. They are mixed with oil, vinegar, salt, a little sugar and finely chopped onions.

Tomato salad, potato salad and green bean salad mixed are a very good combination.

CARROT SALAD (Karottensalat)

R a w carrots are grated coarsely, mixed with a little oil, lemon juice, salt and pepper.

Salads as entrées or individual meals:

EGG SALAD (Eisalat)

Hard boiled eggs are quartered, and served with a dressing of oil, vinegar, salt and pepper. They look their best on a bed of lettuce and are sprinkled with plenty of freshly grated horseradish.

EGG SALAD WITH MAYONNAISE

Into a mayonnaise cut boiled potatoes (about 1 lb) 5 hard boiled eggs, 5 peeled tomatoes, chives. Mix carefully and arrange on lettuce.

SAUSAGESALAD (Knackwurstsalat)

This is a special kind of sausage, in between a bolony and a frankfurter. I suggest preparing it with sliced bolony or cooked and skinned sliced frankfurters. Arrange the sausage slices on a plate, sprinkle chopped onions over it and pour a mixture of oil, vinegar and a little water on top.

SAUSAGESALAD AND HARDBOILED EGGS

Is the same as the above with hardboiled sliced eggs added. The same salad can be varied with peeled and sliced tomatoes or with green beans, potatoes and tomatoes.

BEEF SALAD

Boiled lean beef is cut into fine strips and put into a dressing of finely chopped onions mixed with a teaspoon of mustard, two table-spoons of oil, salt, pepper, a pinch of sugar, 1 tablespoon of vinegar.

MEAT SALAD

½ lb Roast lean meat (Pork or Veal)
½ lb lean boiled beef

½ lb boiled sliced potatoes
5 pickled cucumbers
chopped chives

The cucumbers are peeled and chopped, the meat is cut finely and everything is mixed with a dressing consisting of: 3 tablespoons mayonnaise, 1 tablespoon vinegar, 1 teaspoon french mustard, salt, pepper. Chopped capers and chives can be added.

FISH SALAD (Fischsalat)

½ lb steamed white fish
5 ozs cooked diced carrots
3 tomatoes

3 hardboiled eggs
5 ozs green sliced cooked beans
5 ozs peeled sliced potatoes

Mix six tablespoons of mayonnaise with pepper, salt, a little lemon juice, a teaspoon of french mustard. Mix the cut and diced carrots, beans, potatoes and the fish with this, garnish with hard boiled eggs and tomatoes.

CHICKEN SALAD (Hühnersalat)

1 lb of cooked Chickenmeat	1 root Celery
1 apple	5 tomatoes (for decoration)
5 tomatoes	3 - 4 pickled cucumbers (peeled)

In a bowl of mayonnaise, mix the peeled and sliced tomatoes, the diced chickenmeat, the peeled and finely chopped pickles, the shredded celery. Arrange surrounded by hardboiled egg and tomato quarters.

CHICKEN AND HAM SALAD

½ lb lean boiled ham	½ of a cooked chicken
½ lb boiled potatoes	3 - 4 pickled cucumbers
1 small tin of tiny green peas	

In a mayonnaise mix the chickenmeat, the ham (both cut into strips), the peeled and chopped cucumbers, the green peas with the sliced potatoes. Serve on a bed of lettuce.

HAM AND TONGUE SALAD (Italian style)

Tomatoes, peeled and sliced, chopped capers, chopped chives, diced ham, diced tongue, peeled pickled cucumbers, a few boiled potatoes are mixed with a mayonnaise, to which you have added a little french mustard and a little tomato purée.

Soups

CLEAR SOUP (Klare Suppe)

The best of all clear broths is real Beef broth, and this is the soup eaten most throughout Austria; almost every day in fact, and if you think that boring, let me go further and tell you that my Grand-mother's old cookery book lists 185 ways of serving it! But don't worry, I'm not going to list them all here, only the best, and those which at the same time don't give too much work. But first let me start with the soup itself.

WHITE BEEF BROTH (Klare reine Rindsuppe)

3 pints water
1 lb beef bones (chopped into convenient pieces)
½ oz salt (1½ tablespoons)
2 ozs beef liver
2 ozs carrot
2 ozs parsley root

1 oz celery root
2 ozs onion
1½ lbs beef (this can be a cheaper cut from an older animal)
2 leeks, 2 tomatoes, a little cauli-flower — are optional.

Wash and clean vegetables, cut into fairly large pieces. Wash the meat quickly in cold water, just a rinse under the fawcett (tap). Scald the bones and rinse in cold water. Cut the liver into small pieces and place together with the vegetables and bones, the water and the salt into a large saucepan, and bring to the boil. Now put the meat into the soup and bring to the boil once more, then quickly lower the flame, cover the saucepan and keep over small flame for about 1½ hours (or until meat is tender). There are many people who say that the meat should be put into the pot at once with the other ingredients, but I would advise this only if you don't mind a loss of flavour in the meat in favour of more in the soup. If there is any grey scum forming on the soup leave it (but only if you

are certain that you have washed the vegetables well!) as it is only the protein forming.

Now strain the soup, leave to cool and take off surplus fat. To get the soup quite clear, it can be poured through a fine cloth put over a sieve, or beat the white of an egg with a tablespoon of cold water and lower this carefully into the strained and boiling soup. Lower heat at once and leave soup for ten minutes over very low flame, and all impurities will sink to the bottom of the pot.

BROWN BEEF BROTH (Braune klare Rindsuppe)

The same ingredients as before.

Clean vegetables, bones, beef, liver in the same way. Put 1 oz of lard into a frying pan and fry the cut vegetables, liver and the chopped bones until brown, transfer into soup saucepan, rinsing out the frying pan with a little of the water. Now add rest of the water and when this boils add the meat. Proceed the same way as in previous recipe.

For ways of using the meat of these soups see under Beef. The vegetables are usually never served with the soup, as there is always the possibility of bone splinters being among them, and in any case, all their nourishment has already gone into the soup.

Now some of the 185 ways of serving your clear beef broth (they are used either for brown or white soup, it is just a matter of taste).

BOUILLON AND EGG (Bouillon mit Ei)

This is the simplest method: just put a broken egg into each soup cup or plate and cover with the hot soup, which will just set the outside part of the egg, and each person stirs it for himself. Some people prefer the yolk of the egg, instead of the whole.

WITH POACHED EGG (Pochiertes Ei)

As in the Bouillon, an egg is placed at the bottom of the soup cup, only this time it is poached first, and if liked, a little finely chopped chives can be sprinkled on the soup before serving.

NOODLES (Nudeln)

The thin vermicelli variety are used, which you can buy ready-made. It is better to boil them in water separately, and then strain and add to the soup. In case you want to be an old-fashioned housewife and try your hand at home-made noodles, I'll give you the recipe:

8 ozs flour   *2 tablespoons water*
2 eggs   *pinch of salt*

On a wooden pastry board, sift your flour with the salt, making a small mound in the middle of the board. On top of this mound make a shallow hole into which you put the eggs and the water. Fill the flour in from all sides and knead well, very well! Make into a ball, then roll out as thinly as possible. Leave to dry for half an hour and cut into fairly wide strips as equally as possible. Put one on top of the other and then cut as thinly as you can. Leave noodles to dry on pastry board. They can be made in advance and kept in a dry place for some time until needed.

HALF INCH SQUARES OF PASTA (Fleckerl)

Are made of the same pastry only cut into tiny regular squares.

SEMOLINA NOCKERL (Grießnockerl)

2 tablespoons of lard or butter (oil cannot be used in this recipe)
2 eggs

8 tablespoons of semolina,
pinch of salt

Cream the fat, gradually add the salt, the eggs and the semolina and leave for at least an hour. Now dip a teaspoon into the hot soup (to prevent sticking), and with it take out spoonfuls of the mixture and drop into the boiling soup one after the other. When all the Nockerl are in, turn the flame quite low and simmer very gently for 20 minutes.

WITH RICE (Reis)

Boiled rice is added to the soup, the quantity depends on taste, i. e., whether or not you like the soup thick with it. Chopped parsley is sprinkled on top before serving.

WITH "EINGETROPFTEM"

This means "dropped in". Into 2½ pints of clear soup which should be boiling, the following batter is dropped in from a jug which has a lip, and while doing this, agitate the jug. The "Eingetropfte" should only boil up once and should be served immediately.

Batter:
2½ ozs flour (½ cup)

1 egg
2 - 3 tablespoons milk

All these ingredients are mixed well together with a pinch of salt.

WITH TINY PROFITEROLES (Brandteigkrapferl)

See the recipe for "Profiteroles" under "Cakes and Pastries". Form tiny ones, as small as possible, bake as directed and serve separately with the soup.

WITH FRIDATTEN (pancakes, cut up)

You can use your own favourite pancake recipe, or one from this book which you will find under Desserts. Roll the pancakes (without any filling) and cut into noodles as thinly as you can and put into the cups or soup tureen before pouring the soup on - they should not be put into the boiling soup as they become soggy. You can also add a little chopped parsley to the batter.

WITH NOCKERL (Nockerl)

3 ozs butter (6 tablespoons) *2 egg yolks*
2 tablespoons milk *5 ozs flour*
salt

Beat the butter well, add the yolks, the milk and the salt, then add the stiffly beaten white of egg which you have mixed lightly with the flour. With a teaspoon, form small Nockerl which you put into plenty of boiling salted water. Simmer for 10 minutes. Strain and put into clear soup.

You can also serve the soup with the following dumplings (use the recipes given under Dumplings, only making them much smaller):

with Semmelknödel, with Speckknödel,
with Tirolerknödel, with Bröselknödel, with Potatodumplings.

WITH RICE AND SAVOY CABBAGE (Reis und Kohl)
(This applies to brown clear soup only)

For 2½ pints of clear soup, allow 3 ozs of finely shredded cabbage fried in a little fat, and 2 ozs of rice which you have mixed with 1 oz of grated cheese, and also fried until it is soft. Add cabbage and rice to soup just before serving.

WITH LIVER DUMPLINGS (Leberknödel)

5 ozs liver (it can be beef liver)	2 rolls
2 ozs fat (4 tablespoons)	1 oz onion
2 ozs breadcrumbs (6 tablespoons)	spoon of chopped parsley
salt, pepper, marjoram (a pinch)	1 egg

Put the liver through the mincer, then the two rolls (which you have first soaked in a little milk and squeezed out), add the onion which you have fried golden in the fat, together with the chopped parsley. Add the egg, the breadcrumbs, salt, pepper, marjoram. Let the mixture stand for half an hour and then make into small dumplings. If too soft, add a few more breadcrumbs, put into boiling soup, turn the flame low and simmer for about ten minutes.

LIVER RICE (Leberreis)

The ingredients are the same as in previous recipe. Put through a grater or a perforated spoon by forcing the mixture into the boiling soup with a wooden spoon so that small "rice" is formed. Then simply boil up quickly and serve.

SPRING SOUP (Frühlingsgemüsesuppe)

For 2½ pints of clear beef broth you need about 1 lb of mixed vegetables. Take the youngest and choicest for preference, cut into cubes of approximately equal size and toss in 2 tablespoons of butter over a low flame for a few minutes, then cover and simmer until soft in their own juice. If needed, add a little of the clear soup. When vegetables are done, put into soup and serve. You can use broken small sprigs of cauliflower, asparagus tips, green peas, young carrots, young beans etc.

WITH SEMOLINA (Griess)

Into 2½ pints of clear boiling soup, 2 ozs of semolina (¹/₈ cup) are added gradually while stirring all the time. Simmer slowly until semolina is cooked.

CLEAR CHICKEN SOUP (Klare Hühnersuppe)

1 not-so-young boiling fowl	*1 carrot, 1 parsley root*
1 medium celery root	*salt*
3 pints water	

(The flavour is improved if you add 3 ozs of boiling beef)

Put the fowl (cut into two halves) with its liver, stomach and the vegetables into the pot, together with 3 pints of water. Bring to the boil and simmer for two hours until meat is soft. Strain and clear as you would beef broth. Cut the meat, the liver and stomach (do try it, it's very good) into little pieces and serve in the soup. A little vermicelli can be added if liked. You can also serve the soup with vermicelli only, together with the stomach and liver cut up, and use the meat of the fowl for any of the recipes using boiled chicken under "Game and Poultry".

THICK CHICKEN SOUP (Legierte Hühnersuppe)

The same amounts and method as in previous recipe.
Now make an "Einbrenn" of 4 ozs butter with 3 ozs flour, and add a teaspoon of chopped parsley. Then add the strained soup and the meat cut up as before. This can also be served with rice instead of the meat, or small Bröselknödel. It can be improved by adding sprigs of cauliflower, tiny peas and or asparagus tips, sautéed mushrooms etc.
This brings us to the thick soups. They can all be made with a beef broth (a real one of course), but they are just as nice if you use the vegetable water with a good beef cube. I shall refer to this as stock from now on.

Now two soups which are neither clear nor thick — they can be made either with beef broth, or if they are made with stock, they are called "mock soups".

FRIED SEMOLINA SOUP (Grießsuppe)

3 pints stock
2 ozs coarse semolina (6 tablespoons)
2 tablespoons butter or lard

chopped chives or
chopped parsley
salt, pepper

Melt the fat, adding the semolina, and fry until brown. Now add the stock, salt and pepper, and cook gently for about half an hour. Serve with the chopped chives or parsley sprinkled on top. The soup may be improved by adding sautéed mushrooms or an egg can be stirred into the soup. If you have a weakness for onions, a medium sized one can be fried with the semolina.

PANADLSOUP (Panadlsuppe)

3 stale rolls
2 egg yolks

1 cup of cream
2 pints of stock

Cut rolls into small pieces and put into saucepan with the stock. Cook until all the rolls have dissolved (you can speed this up by beating with an egg whisk). Salt and pepper are now added and the cream which you have beaten well with the 2 egg yolks. Pour this into the boiling soup, stirring all the time. Add a lump of butter before serving.

VEGETABLE SOUP (Gemüsesuppe)

1 carrot, 1 medium root of celery, a few sprigs of cauliflower, 1 tablespoon of green peas, a few sliced mushrooms, a few asparagus tips, in fact any vegetables in season can be used and varied. 3 - 4 cubed potatoes, 2 tablespoons of flour, 3 pints of stock, 2 tablespoons fat.

Cut all the vegetables, then fry in the fat stirring all the time. Now add the flour, fry until light brown, add the stock, pepper and salt and bring to the boil. When vegetables are almost done add the diced potatoes, and when these are done, serve.

CARRAWAY SEED SOUP (Kümmelsuppe)

2 ozs butter (4 tablespoons)   *1 tablespoon carraway seeds*
2 ozs flour (6 tablespoons)   *2 pints of stock (4 cups)*

Melt the fat and stir in the flour, fry until golden brown. Add the stock and the carraway seeds; simmer for 30 minutes. Serve with small cubes of toast (which you have fried in a little butter) in a separate dish.

POTATO SOUP (Erdäpfelsuppe)

1 carrot, 1 medium root of celery, 1 medium onion, 1 clove of garlic (optional), 1 tablespoon of flour, 1 oz fat, 6 large potatoes. 2 pints of stock (4 cups), salt, pepper and a pinch of marjoram. Put all the vegetables (cut into small pieces) together with the peeled and diced potatoes, the pepper, salt and marjoram with the stock into a saucepan and boil until vegetables are soft. Now put through a sieve. Fry the flour in the fat until lightly browned, now add the soup gradually, stirring all the time. Simmer for another 10 minutes, add a knob of butter and serve sprinkled with chives.

CAULIFLOWER SOUP (Karfiolsuppe)

1 large cauliflower (about 1½ lbs)   *3 ozs flour (9 tablespoons)*
3 ozs butter (6 tablespoons)   *5 pints water*

Divide the cauliflower so that the best sprigs are kept separately.

The rest, including the leaves (if they are not too coarse) and the bottom part, are cooked in the stock or salted water until soft, then they are put through a sieve. Fry the flour in the fat and when light brown, add the soup gradually. Bring to the boil and now add the sprigs of cauliflower which you have kept aside. Simmer until these are soft and serve with small pieces of toast fried in butter.

SAVOY CABBAGE SOUP (Kohlsuppe)

2 heads of Savoy cabbage	*1 oz flour (3 tablespoons)*
3 ozs butter (6 tablespoons)	*2 pints stock*
3 - 4 large cooked potatoes (cut	*2 pairs Frankfurters*
into small cubes)	*salt and pepper*

Cook the cabbage which you have cut into fairly large pieces in the stock. When done, strain and pass through a sieve, fry the flour in the fat golden brown, add the soup gradually and cook for ten minutes on low flame. Add the peeled and sliced frankfurters, the diced potatoes, and serve.

LEEK SOUP (Poréesuppe)

4 - 5 large leeks	*3 - 4 boiled and cubed potatoes*
3 ozs fat (6 tablespoons)	*(optional)*
2 ozs flour (6 tablespoons)	

Wash and shred the leeks finely, sauté in the fat, add the flour, fry until golden, now add the stock, cook slowly until leeks are soft. Add the potatoes or serve with fried cubes of toast.

SOUR CREAM SOUP (Saure Milchsuppe)

½ pint of sour milk (1 cup)
3 - 4 boiled potatoes cut into
  small cubes
1 tablespoon flour

½ pint sour cream (½ cup)
2½ pints water
1 teaspoon carraway seeds

Cook the carraway seeds in the salted water for about 10 minutes. Now lower flame as much as you can and stir in gradually (whisking all the time) the sour milk which you have mixed well with the flour. Now bring to the boil and add the sour cream, turn off quickly; it should not be allowed to boil again once the sour cream has been added. Now add the boiled and cubed potatoes and serve. In some parts of the country, a hard boiled egg is put into the soup — one for each person. If liked, chopped dill may also be added to the soup, and if so, this should be done at the same time as the sour milk and flour.

CHEESE SOUP (Käsesuppe)

2 ozs butter (4 tablespoons)
3 pints stock (6 cups)
2 ozs cooked maccaroni (cut
  small pieces)

finely cut chives.
1 oz flour (3 tablespoons)
3 ozs grated cheese (9 tablespoons)

Fry the flour lightly in the fat. Add the stock or water, now boil over a low flame for about half an hour, stir in the grated cheese, simmer for ten more minutes, then add the cooked and cut maccaroni (or any other small noodles) and serve with chopped chives.

GREEN PEA SOUP (Erbsensuppe)

½ lb shelled green peas
1 oz butter (2 tablespoons)

2 pints water
1 oz flour (3 tablespoons)

Cook the peas in salted water. When almost soft add the flour which you have fried lightly in the fat, stirring well so that no lumps form. Now put in Butternockerl (see recipe under Clear Soups).

114

BEAN SOUP (Bohnensuppe)

3 ozs white beans	2 pints water
2 ozs onions	1 oz fat (2 tablespoons)
1 oz flour (3 tablespoons)	1 large onion
3 ozs cooked diced ham	salt, pepper

Cook the beans until soft. Fry the onion golden brown, now add the flour and when this is also brown, add to the beans and stock, simmer for ten minutes, then put through a sieve. Now add the diced ham and serve with onion rings which you have fried in a little fat.

Note: The above, as well as cabbage soup can be made with stock obtained by cooking ham. Take care not to oversalt when using this! Also potato soup and carraway soup can be made with this if the bacon-ham flavour is liked. For all the other thick soups, stock obtained from veal bones can be used.

LENTIL SOUP (Linsensuppe)

The same as before, except that lentils are substituted instead of beans, and Frankfurters are cut into it instead of ham. Leave out the onion and serve with small pieces of toast fried in butter. In both of these soups one can keep back either a few beans or lentils when they are cooked, and before they are put through the sieve, so that they can be added to the soup later.

ASPARAGUS SOUP (Spargelsuppe)

1 lb asparagus of a lesser quality
2 ozs butter (4 tablespoons)
1 oz flour (3 tablespoons)

2½ pints stock
a few asparagus tips (they can be tinned)

Cook the asparagus in the stock until soft, then put through a sieve. Fry the flour in the fat lightly, and to this add the soup gradually. Cook for ten minutes, then add the asparagus tips. Serve with fried toast. This soup can be improved by adding the yolk of an egg beaten with 1 cup of cream before serving.

TOMATO SOUP (Paradeissuppe)

1 oz fat (1 tablespoon)
2 lbs tomatoes (or the tinned equivalent)
1 oz flour (3 tablespoons)

1 teaspoon sugar
2 pints water
salt, pepper

Cook the tomatoes and put through a sieve. Fry the flour in the fat as normally, then add the soup, sugar, salt. Bring to the boil and simmer for ten minutes. If liked, some sour cream or sweet cream can be added, also a drop of lemon juice. Boiled rice or small maccaroni are tasty in this soup, but it can also be served without anything.

MUSHROOM SOUP (Schwammerlsuppe)

5 ozs mushrooms
3 ozs flour (¾ cup)
salt, pepper

2 ozs butter (4 tablespoons)
3 pints stock

Slice the mushrooms and fry in the butter; add the flour and when this is slightly brown, add the stock and some chopped parsley. Bring to the boil and simmer for about half an hour. If liked, half a cup of cream can be added, but certainly a knob of fresh butter before serving. Small Bröselknödel or tiny Semmelknödel are usually served in this soup. They can be cooked either in this or in salted water. (For recipe see under "Beilagen".)

Entrées

LIPTAUER

This is not really an Entrée, but a cheese, so into which chapter should I put it? But include it I must, as it is so delicious!

½ lb cream cheese (1 cup)
  slightly less of butter
  (approx. ¾ cup)
1 teaspoon chopped capers
1 teaspoon chopped chives
1 teaspoon chopped parsley
1 teaspoon french mustard

1 chopped anchovy
pinch powdered carraway seeds
pinch pepper
1 teaspoon very finely chopped
  onions
salt, enough paprika to make the
  mixture a pleasant pink.

All the ingredients are put together into a deep bowl and mixed very thoroughly. It tastes delicious on toast, brown bread, rolls or with a glass of beer and radishes, in fact it tastes delicious anyway! In the Austrian restaurants, this dish is usually served unmixed: on a plate you are given a little cream cheese, a piece of butter, and this is surrounded by small quantities of the other ingredients. I once came across a young American who had ordered this, and he didn't know that one is supposed to mix it oneself at the table. He started therefore to eat everything bit by bit, and by the time I got to his table to explain, he had already finished more than half, so there was not much point in mixing the rest, but I'm afraid that his taste for Liptauer must have been spoilt forever!

HAM ROLLS AND HORSERADISH CREAM CHEESE
(Schinkenrollen mit Kren)

The ham should be lean and pink. For each person allow one or two slices of ham according to appetite, and two to three tablespoons of cream cheese, depending on the size of the ham slice, which should be very thin. Again to each person allow one heaped teaspoon of freshly grated horseradish or two of the kind which you buy ready mixed. When you have measured all the ingredients, put the cream cheese in a bowl, mix thoroughly with the horseradish, pepper and salt. To moisten, add a few tablespoons of mayonnaise, the number of these depends on the quantity altogether prepared. Now spread each ham slice thickly with the mixture and roll together as you would a swiss roll. Place them side by side on a bed of lettuce leaves and garnish with chopped aspic.

TROUT IN ASPIC JELLY (Forelle in Aspik)

Trout are cooked as carp (see under Fish) in aspic jelly. They are cooked whole with just the entrails removed. Take care that the water doesn't boil, you will find they are done when the eyes come out as hard white balls. They should remain quite straight. Lift them out carefully, and either arrange them whole or skinned and filleted on a platter, garnish with lemon slices and spoon liquid aspic jelly over them until they are quite covered. Serve with a mayonnaise sauce.

ASPARAGUS CREME (Spargelcrême)

¼ pint (½ cup) milk
4 egg yolks and 1 egg

5 ozs tinned or freshly cooked asparagus

Drain the asparagus, and put through a sieve, so that you obtain a thick crême. Mix this well with the egg yolks and the whole egg and a pinch of salt. Butter small forms (as a guide to size, they should be large enough to hold the contents of half a normal cup), if you don't have any of this size use black coffee cups. Butter and flour them lightly, then fill in with the mixture. Into a shallow casserole put a little water, bring to the boil, and insert the moulds. Cook for ¾ of an hour, but watch that no water gets into the moulds. Turn out onto a plate on which you have put some chopped lettuce, garnish with chopped aspic, asparagus tips and mayonnaise.

118

CHICKEN IN ASPIC (Huhn in Aspik)

Use the meat of a boiled or roasted fowl. Line a mould with aspic (see under Essentials), garnish with skinned and sliced pickled cucumber and sliced stuffed olives. Now put the chicken into the mould alternatively with the cool liquid aspic. Leave to set. Turn out onto a "platform" of vegetable salad (see under Salads), serve with mayonnaise sauce.

CHICKEN IN MAYONNAISE ASPIC (Huhn in Mayonnaiseaspik)

Is prepared exactly as above, using half mayonnaise to half aspic, and is turned out onto a bed of shredded lettuce; garnish with chopped aspic. Serve with various salads.

HAM CORNETS (Schinkenstarnitzel)

A "Starnitzel" really means a cornet, and is a paperbag which grocers form out of a piece of paper, you occasionally still see them do it over here.

You take a large lean piece of ham, make it into a cornet and fill it with one of the following fillings. Arrange on a bed of lettuce, preferably on a round one with all the cornet points meeting in the middle.

Liver filling: Lightly fried calf or goose liver is put through a sieve mixed with half its quantity of butter, salt and pepper are added to taste, also 1 teaspoon of brandy.

Ham filling: Lean ham is put through the mincer, then through a sieve, half the quantity of butter is added, salt and french mustard — a little mayonnaise can also be included.

Chicken filling: Meat of a roasted or boiled fowl is put through the mincer, then through a sieve, half the quantity of butter is added, some mayonnaise and seasoning.

They can also be filled with any of the following salads:
Ham and tongue, Chicken and ham, Egg, Mayonnaise and Vegetable Salad.

(All of these you will find under Salads.)

119

STUFFED EGGS (Gefüllte Eier)

Allowing one egg for each person (if used as an Entrée, or two if it should be part of a cold supper), the eggs are hardboiled (ten minutes)then cooled, peeled and cut into half, which can be done lengthways or across. Whichever way you do it, it is necessary to cut a tiny piece off the part where the egg should stand. Arrange the eggs on a bed of shredded lettuce or vegetable salad (see "Salads"). They can be covered with a thick mayonnaise or the mayonnaise can be served separately, but this is optional.

For the filling: Take out the yolks carefully, put them into a basin, mix them thoroughly with a fork, then add as much creamed butter or mayonnaise as is necessary to get a smooth mixture, nearly double the quantity of the yolks. For flavoring add: finely chopped ham, finely ground sardines or anchovies, lightly fried liver put through a sieve, or a spoonful of caviar, or chopped chives and parsley.

Fill this into the egg white shells, it should form a small mound which you can decorate with your fork, or by piping mayonnaise on top, by adding chopped chives or sprinkling caviar.

Any of these above mentioned fillings and also the ones I've given you for the ham cornet can be put into

STUFFED TOMATOES:

The tomatoes are peeled (but only if they are very firm)see under Essentials for method. The stalk end is cut off, the pulp is taken out carefully with a small spoon (you can use this inner part for soup or sauces). Now put in any of the fillings mentioned for the Stuffed Eggs or the Schinkenstarnitzel. A delicious filling is also: cream cheese to which you have added mayonnaise, chopped chives, chopped radishes and hardboiled chopped eggs.

SIMPLE LIVER PASTE (Einfache Leberpastete)

1 lb of calf, pig, chicken or
    gooseliver
3 eggs
1 medium sized onion

1 tablespoon sherry,
    salt, pepper, a pinch of paprika
2 tablespoons butter

Slice the onions, fry in some oil (about 2 tablespoons) add the liver to this when the onions turn golden. The liver should be cut into slices and then into smaller pieces. Fry quickly, stirring. When the liver is done, pour the eggs which you have scrambled with a little milk over this, allow to set. Now put all this through the mincer (twice if necessary) add the butter, sherry and the spices. Form into a block or pudding shape, garnish with parsley and aspic. This tastes excellent as an entrée served with hot wafer thin toast, but also makes a very good sandwich spread and a filling for savory puff pastry (hot or cold) or profiteroles.

EGGS IN HORSERADISH MAYONNAISE
(Eier in Krenmayonnaise)

To each person allow one mediumboiled egg — they should not be hard! Into a mayonnaise (see under Essentials, Sauces) stir liberal quantities of freshly grated horseradish, put into a glass bowl and add the cooled and peeled eggs. (Poached eggs can also be used as an alternative.)

EGGS IN GREEN MAYONNAISE (Frühlingseier)

The same method as above, except that in this case two tablespoons of spinach either parboiled or raw (which has been put through a sieve) is added to the mayonnaise — the quantity allows for six persons. Again medium boiled eggs are put into the mayonnaise. Sprinkle with chopped chives and chopped parsley.

EGGS IN HAM MAYONNAISE (Schinkeneier)

Allow one medium boiled egg to each person, one heaped teaspoon of very finely chopped lean ham to each two tablespoons of mayonnaise. Mix well, and insert the eggs in the mayonnaise.

EGGS IN PINK MAYONNAISE (Eier in Tomatenmayonnaise)

One generous tablespoon of tomato purée for each cup of mayonnaise, mix well, and insert one medium boiled egg into this. Garnish with tomato quarters or shrimps.

MUSHROOMS IN ASPIC (Schwammerln in Aspik)

Cut medium sized mushrooms into fairly thick slices, cook them briskly in some water with a drop of lemon. Drain and cool. Line a mould with aspic (see under Essentials), put in a layer of mushrooms, then more aspic, and wait until this is set. Again more mushrooms, aspic and so on until the moulds are filled. Turn out and garnish.

Almost all vegetables can be prepared in this way: peas, asparagus, artichoke fonds, cauliflower are cooked first, tomatoes can be used raw. You can also make a mixture of vegetables, using half aspic and half mayonnaise. These vegetables can be made either in individual moulds or in one large one. They are served rather as an accompaniment to any cold meat or any of the cold egg recipes which I've given you, than as an entrée on their own. But they will certainly add glamour to your cold entrée or buffet, as they are so attractive and at the same time so easy to make.

Any cold meat, ham or tongue, fish, small pieces of lobster, shrimps by themselves or mixed with suitable vegetables and combined wtih aspic in a mould, makes a quickly prepared entrée on its own or as an addition to a cold meal.

LIVER PATÉ (Leberpastete)

1½ lbs veal or pig's liver
1 roll soaked in milk
1 teaspoon Worcester sauce

¾ lb (1¼ cups) butter
1 tablespoon madeira wine or
  sherry
salt, pepper, a tiny pinch of curry

Put the liver cut into slices into a bowl of milk for an hour. Drain and dry thoroughly, fry slowly in a little oil until well done — there should not be a trace of blood. The roll which has been soaked in the milk is now squeezed out and put through the mincer, then the liver, do it twice if necessary as it must be quite smooth. Now mix this thoroughly with the creamed butter, the madeira, Worcester sauce and the spices. Form into a brick and put into the ice. It looks more attractive if brushed with cool liquid aspic. Garnish with chopped aspic.

PORK BRAWN (Haussulz)

1 pig's trotter
1 lb lean stewing pork
1 large onion
2 to 3 carrots

½ a pig's head (without brains
    as they can be used for some-
    thing else)
bayleaves, peppercorns
some celery root
2 cloves

Cover the meat in a large saucepan with 4 pints of water. Add all
seasonings, bring to the boil and simmer for about 3 hours until the
meat is quite soft. Now strain the liquid into a bowl. Take the
meat off the bones and cut as finely as you can. Remove all fat of
the liquid, put meat back into saucepan, bring to the boil; put into
a mould (which has been moistened) and leave to set, stirring
occasionally so that the meat is mixed well with the jelly. It is best
to leave it overnight. You can add some smoked tongue or ham,
to the meat, cut into small pieces. Turn out and garnish with
gherkins, hardboiled eggs and serve with a dressing of chopped
onions in a little vinegar and oil.

BOILED BEEF IN ASPIC (Rindfleisch in Aspik)

Put a lean piece of boiling beef into a saucepan with the usual vegetables, and rather less water. When the meat is quite soft, take
out, clear the soup (see under Soups) and pluck the meat (rather
than cut it) into small pieces, you will find it best to use two forks
for this. Return this to the cleared soup, and bring to the boil again,
simmer for another hour until it becomes quite thick, then pour
into a mould which has been moistened, and put into the ice-box.
Turn out, garnish with hardboiled eggs and tomatoes. You can
also add peeled gherkins cut into fine strips to the mixture before
pouring it into the mould.

These following Entrées you will find listed in other parts of the book:

Under Salads:
Egg Salad (Eiersalat) - with and without Mayonnaise — Chicken Salad (Hühnersalat) — Sausage Salad (Wurstsalat) - with and without eggs — Beef Salad (Rindfleischsalat) — Meat Salad (Fleischsalat) — Chicken and Ham Salad (Hühner- und Schinkensalat) — Fish Salad (Fischsalat) — Ham and Tongue Salad (Schinken- und Zungensalat) — Chicken Salad (Hühnersalat).

Under Fish:
Carp in Aspic (Gesulzter Karpfen) — Cold Paprika Carp (Kalter Paprikafisch) — Herring Salad I and II (Heringsalat) — Fish Mayonnaise — Fish in Aspic — Marinated Fried Fish.

Under Vegetables:
Mushrooms and Eggs, Cauliflower and Ham, Stuffed Tomatoes, Steamed Spinach pudding, Vegetable pudding.

Under Offal:
Fried brains with or without eggs, Braingnocchi (Hirnnockerln), Brain pudding, Pancakes with Brainfilling, Brains on Toast, Kidneys and Brains.

Under Plain Dishes:
Steamed and Baked Ham pudding.

HOT ENTREES

PROFITEROLES WITH SAVOURY FILLINGS
(Brandteigkrapferl mit salziger Fülle)

2 ozs butter (¹/₃ cup)   *½ pint water*
3 eggs   *pinch salt*
1 cup flour

Bring the butter, the water and the salt to the boil in a saucepan, add the flour stirring on a low flame (take care it must not burn) until you have obtained a thick paste, it should look greasy, and is ready when it comes away from the spoon easily. Take away from heat, stir until cold, then add the eggs one by one, stirring well. Leave this for at least three quarters of an hour. Now butter a baking sheet and with the help of two teaspoons dipped in egg white, form little heaps well apart. Brush with egg white and sprinkle with one of the following: carraway seeds, a pinch of paprika or poppyseeds. (You can sprinkle some with one, and some with the other and so on.) Warm the oven, put the sheet in and bake in a medium hot oven for ten minutes without opening the oven door. Then open, turn the heat off and leave the Profiteroles to cool in the warm oven.

When cool, make a slit and fill with any one of the following fillings, and before serving, put for a few minutes into a medium hot oven.

1.) 1 cup of stiffly whipped cream to which you add half a cup of grated cheese, a pinch of salt and a pinch of paprika.

2.) About 5 ozs of fried liver (chicken, goose or calf) are put through a sieve and then mixed with an egg yolk, salt, pepper.

3.) 3 hardboiled eggs are chopped and mixed with 1 tablespoon of mayonnaise, 2 tablespoons of chopped ham.

4.) 3 - 4 ozs of braised veal are put through the mincer, mixed with 1 chopped anchovy, 1 teaspoon of chopped capers, 1 tablespoon of mayonnaise, 1 teaspoon of sherry.

5.) To 1 cup of Béchamel (see under Essentials) add 2 tablespoons of grated cheese, 1 chopped hardboiled egg, 1 - 2 tablespoons of chopped smoked tongue.

6.) To 1 cup of chopped chicken add 2 tablespoons of mayonnaise and a few chopped olives.

Liptauer, ham, liver, chicken filling (the recipes for which you will find in this chapter under Schinkenstarnitzel) can be used. The profiteroles can also be served cold.

GULYASSTRUDEL

Make a Strudelpastry (see under Cakes and Pastries) divide the quantity into two halves. Pull the first half out as described and as thinly as possible, now brush with melted butter, fold together, brush again. Lard a shallow square baking tin (lard or oil is used here as butter burns easily), and to the size of the tin fit the folded Strudelpastry. Now the filling is put on, about one and a half inches thick. The filling consists of beef, pork or veal gulyas which you have prepared the day before (an excellent use for leftover Gulyas). Take out the meat and cut into tiny cubes, return to the gravy and simmer until it has quite a thick consistency. Leave to cool, you should have 1 - 2 cups of gulyas, depending on the size of your tin. Now prepare the second half of the Strudel as before and use to cover the filling. Brush over with melted butter and bake in hot oven. Cut into squares and serve hot.

BRAINSTRUDEL (Hirnstrudel)

Is prepared the same way, fried veal brain (see under Offal) being substituted for the Gulyas.

MUSHROOMSTRUDEL (Schwammerlstrudel)

Is again the same, only this time the filling consists of sautéed mushrooms (see under Vegetables).

OMELETTE

Here is a basic recipe which an be used with a variety of fillings:

1 oz flour (¼ cup)	*3 eggs*
1 oz butter (2 heaped tablespoons)	*½ cup milk*

Cook the milk with the butter, stir in the flour, when you have a thick paste, take away from heat and stir in one egg yolk after the other. Now whisk the egg whites stiffly and add to the mixture carefully. Bake in a buttered omelette pan in the hot oven. Fill with any vegetables, for example: peas, peas and carrots, creamed spinach, sautéed mushrooms (see under Vegetables), fried brain, fried chopped liver (see under Offal), chopped ham or tongue.

EGGS IN SOUR CREAM (Rahmeier)

1 cup sour cream	*1 tablespoon butter*
1 teaspoon chopped parsley	*1 tablespoon breadcrumbs*
1 teaspoon chopped chives	*10 eggs*

Into a flat fireproof dish pour the cup of sour cream. This dish should be large enough to hold the 10 eggs (or you can use small individual fireproof dishes, in this case, allow 1 tablespoon of sour cream and 1 egg to each person) which you now slide carefully into the cream. Sprinkle the eggs with the chives, the parsley and lastly the breadcrumbs, drip the melted butter over and put into a hot oven until the eggs are set and a brown crust is formed.

HAM CROISSANTS (Schinkenkipferl)

Puff pastry (see under Cakes and Pastries) is rolled out to the thickness of the back of a knife. Cut into three inch squares and put a teaspoon of chopped ham, which you have mixed with a little butter, into the middle. Roll up and shape like a crescent. Bake in medium hot oven. The Kipferl can be filled with sautéed chopped mushrooms, creamed chopped chickenmeat, chopped or minced fried liver.

SAUSAGES IN PASTRY (Würstel im Teig)

Prepare as previous recipe, putting half a skinned Frankfurter on the square, and roll up. Or take sausage meat out of its skin (by squeezing it out as you would toothpaste), in sausage shape onto each pastry square, roll up as Frankfurters, and bake.

FRIED CHEESE (Gebackener Emmentaler)

Take a good quality gruyère (swiss cheese) cut into slices a quarter of an inch thick. Dip into flour, egg and breadcrumbs as you would a Wiener Schnitzel; fry in fat.

Plain dishes

MAINLY WITHOUT MEAT

In Austria we very often serve "Mehlspeise", which can be a steamed pudding or fruit dumplings, pancakes and many other things, but it is nearly always what we call a "gekochte Mehlspeise" (steamed sweet). As these are usually quite compact and filling, a Lunch will often consist of two courses only. It can be either a soup and then the sweet or one of the Plain dishes, and if it is not too starchy it can be followed by a sweet. In the summer, a salad can be served and the hot sweet is substituted by a cold one. In bygone days, a menu like that would only be served on meatless Friday, whereas on normal days our fathers and grandfathers were familiar with a soup with something very substantial in it, meat with at least two vegetables, dumplings or potatoes, and a sweet to follow! And to think that, in addition, they would have their small Gulyas or Frankfurters at 11 o'clock plus a "Jause" at 4 o'clock consisting of coffee and yeastcakes! And further, if I told you what they ate on a Sunday, you just wouldn't believe me! So I won't tell, but instead I'll give you a few recipes for the simpler Plain dishes.

I   HAM NOODLES (Schinkenfleckerl)

1 lb Fleckerl (or cut noodles)   2 ozs ham
2 ozs butter (4 tablespoons)

Cook the Fleckerl (as in "Beilagen") put into a saucepan with the
melted fat, add the ham which you have cut finely, toss, and serve
with a salad.

II   SCHINKENFLECKERL

1 lb Fleckerl (or any small pasta)   1 pint sour cream
1 oz butter   butter for the fireproof dish
3 egg yolks   8 ozs chopped ham
3 egg whites

Cream the butter with the egg yolks, add the cream, butter a fireproof dish well, now add the ham to the first mixture and the cooked
and rinsed Fleckerln, lastly the stiffly beaten egg whites. Put into
a fireproof dish and then into the oven for about 20 minutes until
nicely browned on top. Serve with a salad.

POTATO GULYAS (Erdäpfelgulyas)

3 ozs fat (6 tablespoons)   1 teaspoon paprika
2 ozs diced bacon   1 tablespoon vinegar
10 ozs chopped onions   3 lbs potatoes

Fry the diced bacon in the fat, add the chopped onions, fry until
golden, add the paprika, the vinegar, salt and the peeled potatoes
(which should be halved or quartered according to size). Cover with
water so that the potatoes are completely covered, and simmer until
they are done. Sliced Frankfurters or similar sausages can be
added before serving.

POTATOES FRIED TYROLEAN STYLE (Tiroler Gröstl)

To one cup of boiled and sliced potatoes, allow one cup of meat cut
into fine strips (it can be beef or pork, boiled or roasted). Two medium sized onions cut into rings, salt, pepper and carraway seeds.
Fry the potatoes in a little fat until golden, add the meat, fry, and
after tossing well, add the fried onion-rings. Serve hot with salad.

FRIED DUMPLINGS WITH EGGS (Knödel mit Ei)

Almost any leftover Knödel (except Potatodumplings) are tasty when sliced, fried in hot fat and with a few scrambled eggs put over them. Leave until eggs are set, then serve with a salad. Semmelknödel are particularly good that way.

POTATO DUMPLINGS WITH CHOPPED HAM OR BACON
(Erdäpfelknödel mit Fleisch)

Use the recipe given in Dumplings, but while making, put in the middle some chopped ham, or any left over meat well chopped up and seasoned. Form dumpling now and continue as in recipe. Serve with Sauerkraut or a salad.

SOUR CREAM POTATOES (Rahmerdäpfel)

2 lbs potatoes
1/2 pint sour cream (1 cup)
1 cup chopped ham

1 1/2 ozs butter (3 tablespoons)
1/2 cup grated cheese
4 - 5 hard boiled eggs

Boil, peel and then slice the potatoes. Butter a fireproof dish liberally, put in a layer of sliced potatoes and sprinkle this with some of the ham, cheese and some sliced hardboiled egg. Top with a few flakes of butter. Now another layer of potatoes and so on. The last layer being of potatoes. Then pour the cream over the dish loosening the potatoes with the end of a spoon, so that the cream infiltrates thoroughly. Top with a little butter and grated cheese, bake in a moderate oven for about 3/4 of an hour till top is golden brown.

TIROLERKNÖDEL (see under Dumplings)

SPECKKNÖDEL (see under Dumplings)

KRAUTFLECKERLN (see under Beilagen)

SAVOURY PANCAKES
GULYAS PANCAKES (Gulyaspalatschinken)

Make pancakes from your own favourite mix or see recipe in this book. Take some Gulyas, extract the meat, and after cutting as finely as possible return to the Gulyas gravy. It should now have a fairly thick consistency. Grease a fireproof dish, put in a pancake, spread with some of the Gulyas, then another pancake and so on until the mixture and pancakes have been used up. Make the last layer a pancake which you top liberally with butter flakes and grated cheese. Put into oven and bake until top is nicely browned. If liked, and when you have some of the Gulyas gravy left over, it can be served separately.

SPINACH PANCAKES (Spinatpalatschinken)

Can either be made (1) with spinach which has been lightly cooked and just tossed in butter - in this case, it is best to put them into a buttered fireproof dish and put in all the pancakes filled with the spinach, and then cover with a Béchamel (see recipe) to which you have added grated cheese. Bake in moderato oven. Or (2) fill the pancakes with spinach done the Austrian way (see recipe) spread the pancakes with the spinach, roll them up and serve at once with hot browned butter and grated parmesan cheese. We also serve a green salad with this.

MUSHROOM PANCAKES (Pilzpalatschinken)

Can be prepared either way, with sautéed mushrooms as the filling.
Other Savoury Pancake fillings:
1. Peas and chopped ham.
2. Chopped liver fried in a little onion.
3. Brains (see recipe under Offal).

GNOCCHI WITH EGGS (Eiernockerl)

Use leftover Nockerl or make them according to either of the two recipes given under "Beilagen". Now melt a good sized piece of butter in a frying pan, roast the Nockerl in this and pour 3 - 4 eggs (which have been mixed well) over this. When eggs are set, serve with a green salad. You will be surprised how delicious this cheap simple dish is!

WOODCHOPPER'S NOCKERL (Holzhackernockerl)

Is made the same way as the above recipe, except that the Nockerl are put into fried onions and sprinkled liberally with grated cheese. Chopped ham can also be added before serving. Again a salad goes very well with this.

STEAMED HAM PUDDING (Schinkenpudding gekocht)

½ *pint milk (1 cup)*
  2 ozs butter (4 tablespoons)
  2 ozs flour (½ cup)

3 eggs
5 ozs chopped ham
salt, pepper, grated nutmeg

Mix the flour with the milk, add the butter and over a very small flame stir until you obtain a thick paste. Take away from the heat, add the egg yolks, salt, pepper, the grated nutmeg and the chopped ham. Lastly beat the egg whites very stiffly and add to the mixture. Butter a pudding basin, sprinkle with breadcrumbs and pour the pudding mixture into this. Boil gently for about half an hour; serve with grated cheese and a salad.

BAKED HAM PUDDING (Schinkenpudding gebacken)

Is the same as above baked in the oven.

Desserts

WARM

As I mentioned at the beginning of the previous chapter, these steamed and baked sweets are usually served as a main course after soup or vegetables or a salad. However, that should not prevent you serving them as a dessert after a meal. They are nearly all simple and easy to make and are delicious! They could prove useful additions to your list of simple light lunches for the children.

Let me begin with one of the most popular and rightly famous ones:

APRICOT DUMPLINGS (Marillenknödel aus Brandteig)

Approx. 1½ lbs apricots	*3 ozs flour (1½ cups)*
½ pint milk (or milk and water)	*2 eggs*
1 oz butter (2 tablespoons)	*pinch of salt*

Put the milk into a saucepan, add the butter and bring to the boil, add the flour, reduce heat considerably and stir with a wooden spoon over a low flame. This paste is ready when it comes away from the sides of the saucepan in a lump, leaving the sides of the saucepan clean. Now stir in one egg after the other, mix well and leave the paste to cool. Then turn out onto a pastryboard, and form into a long sausage shape from which you cut off small slices. The apricots (which you have previously washed and dried) are now put onto the paste roll between your hands, so that each is completely covered — there must be no gaps. When all the dumplings are moulded into shape, they are dropped into a large saucepan with slightly salted boiling water. You will find that they sink to the bottom, so move them carefully to avoid sticking. When they are done, they will rise to the top and then need only about a minute or two more. They must be cooked very gently in a covered saucepan, but with the lid a little ajar. Take out, put in a colander and when they are completely drained, put them into a pan where you have previously prepared the following mixture: 3 ozs of butter are melted, and in this 3 ozs of breadcrumbs are fried golden brown. Now toss the dumplings gently into this, then remove to a heated dish together with the breadcrumbs, sprinkle with sugar and serve.

Sugar must also be served separately at the table.

If the apricots or the plums should be very sour, the stone can be taken out and replaced by a lump of sugar.

The dumplings can be served with a mixture of ground cinnamon and sugar sprinkled over them and with hot melted butter poured on instead of the fried breadcrumbs.

CHERRY DUMPLINGS (Kirschenknödel)

Are made in the same way, substituting two or three cherries in each dumpling instead of an apricot.

PLUM DUMPLINGS (Zwetschkenknödel)

Are also made in the same way, but where possible, use the pointed small variety of plums which we call "Zwetschken" as they are tastier. Plum dumplings taste very good served with a mixture of ground poppyseeds and sugar and hot butter instead of breadcrumbs. There are several other kinds of paste with which the fruit can be covered, for example, there is a potatopaste and a yeastpaste, but I personally find the one I've given you the lightest to eat and the easiest to prepare, so I will spare you the others!

PANCAKES (Palatschinken)

1 pint milk   ½ lb flour (2 cups)
2 eggs   oil for frying

Sift the flour with a pinch of salt into a bowl, then add one egg, some milk; stir well, then add the other egg and the rest of the milk. Leave this batter for about half an hour before using. Put a little oil into frying pan, dipping the pan so that it is completely covered with the fat, and when it is smoking hot pour in some of the batter. Again move the pan so that the batter is evenly spread over the pan. Shake pan a little, and when one side is done, turn over. Keep hot while you use up the rest of the batter. There are many ways of serving these pancakes, but they are usually rolled up with some filling (for savoury fillings see under "Plain Dishes"). They can be spread with jam, preferably Apricot, rolled up, placed side by side on a warmed dish sprinkled with sugar and served at once.
Grated nuts can also be used as stuffing, mixed with sugar, or grated chocolate, also the following

Cream cheese mixture:

1 oz raisins   grated lemon peel
2 egg yolks   2 ozs sugar (⅓ cup)
2 ozs butter (4 tablespoons) ½ lb cream cheese

All ingredients are mixed thoroughly and the pancakes are filled with the mixture. It is advisable to stand the plate with the stuffed pancakes over some boiling water, so that the cheese mixture does not cool the pancakes too much.

I   BAKED PANCAKES (Gebackene Palatschinken)

Are prepared exactly as Cream Cheese pancakes, but after they have been rolled up with the filling, they are put into a buttered fire

proof dish next to each other, and then on top of each other, and are covered with a mixture which is as follows: one cup of sour cream into which you have stirred one tablespoon of sugar and one egg yolk. Put into the oven and bake until top is nicely browned.

II   BAKED PANCAKES

3 ozs raisins   *1 pint milk (2 cups)*
3 ozs sugar (1 cup)   *4 egg yolks*
3 ozs almonds

Make your pancakes in the usual way, grind the almonds (unskinned), clean the raisins, mix nuts and raisins with the sugar and fill pancakes. Roll together, put into buttered fireproof dish and pour the milk which you have mixed with the yolks and a tablespoon of sugar onto the pancakes, put into oven and bake.

APPLE FRITTERS (Apfelspalten)

The same batter as is used for pancakes can also be used for apple fritters. Apples are cored, peeled and cut into rings, they are dipped into the batter which should be fairly thick, and are then fried in hot fat. Put on filterpaper so that the fat is absorbed a little. Serve at once and sprinkle with sugar at the table.

PINEAPPLE FRITTERS (Ananasspalten)

Pineapple slices are treated the same way, they should be put into a little lemon juice for an hour, drained and then put into the batter.

PEAR FRITTERS (Birnen)

Are cored, peeled and cut across or lengthways.

PRUNE FRITTERS

Large prunes are stewed and stoned. In place of the stone insert a blanched almond. Dip into batter. Fry in hot fat and before serving, roll in grated chocolate and sugar.

PLUMS: can be treated the same way, or halved.

APRICOTS: are skinned and halved.

PEACHES: are skinned and halved. (For hints on skinning see under Essentials.)

STRAWBERRIES IN BATTER

Are washed and drained, the stalks being left on. Now roll the strawberries in a little thinned strawberry jam, then in spongecake crumbs, dip into the batter and fry.
All of these should be put on a filterpaper. The addition of a tablespoon of rum to the batter also prevents it from absorbing too much fat.

SWEET NOODLES (Süße Nudeln)

1. Put noodles (the broad type) into plenty of boiling water, cook until just tender (about twenty minutes), they must on no account be too soft. Drain and rinse under running cold water. After draining again, melt plenty of butter in a saucepan (the amount of butter depends on the quantity of the noodles) and toss the noodles into this, they should not get brown, only thoroughly warmed. Serve on a heated deep dish sprinkled with a mixture of ground walnuts and sugar. A bowl of these should be handed round at the table too - they taste delicious!

2. Are prepared as in 1. ground poppyseeds being used with the sugar instead of walnuts.

3. Ground chocolate is used for sprinkling.

4. Breadcrumbs are fried in butter until golden, the noodles are tossed into this, sprinkled with sugar and served with stewed fruit.

5. Semolina is fried in butter and the noodles are tossed into this; when the semolina is golden, then serve with sugar and stewed fruit.

CHEESE NOODLES (Topfennudeln)

3 eggs
3 ozs sugar (1 cup)
3 ozs butter (6 tablespoons)
4 ozs cream cheese
1 oz raisins

1 cup sour cream
½ lemon (the grated rind and the juice are used)
1 lb noodles

The noodles are cooked in the usual way and when rinsed are mixed with the following: The butter is mixed with the sugar, the egg yolks, the cream, the raisins, the lemonjuice, the lemon rind (finely grated). Finally you add the stiffly beaten egg whites, put into buttered fireproof dish and bake for three quarters of an hour.

Now we have a real Viennese dish and a real Viennese word! A "Schmarren" means nothing, literally nothing, and if someone tells you: "Das geht dich einen Schmarren an", you should be slightly offended, for it means "mind your own business!" But if someone invites you to a "Schmarren", you can accept with pleasure, for it will mean one of the three following recipes, and you are sure to like them! And if you try your own hand at them you will see that they are particularly easy to make, absolutely nothing can go wrong, it is in fact, a mere "trifle", and maybe the name stems from that!

EMPEROR'S NOTHING (Kaiserschmarren)

¼ lb flour (1 cup)
½ pint milk (1 cup)
2 eggs
1 oz sugar (2 tablespoons)
2 ozs butter (4 tablespoons)
1 oz raisins (optional)

Mix the sifted flour with milk, add the sugar and the two egg yolks, a tiny pinch of salt and lastly, the stiffly beaten egg whites. Now there are two methods: you heat the oven, butter a fireproof dish liberally, and pour in about one inch of the mixture. When it is lightly browned, turn, brown on the other side and tear into small pieces with two forks. If you like your puddings slightly.

139

softer, then tear it into pieces when it is just slightly browned, don't turn, and just put into oven for a few minutes, the moisture can then evaporate. It is served on a heated plate, sprinkled with Vanilla-sugar and with fruit syrup or stewed fruit.

SEMOLINA SCHMARREN (Grießschmarren)

½ *pint milk (1 cup)*   1 *oz raisins*
½ *lb semolina (¾ cup)*   3 *ozs butter (6 tablespoons)*
 1 *oz sugar (2 tablespoons)*

Bring the milk to the boil, adding half the butter and the sugar. When boiling, add the semolina, sprinkling while stirring all the time. When the mixture is quite thick, cover, take away from heat and leave for ten minutes. Heat the oven, butter a fireproof dish liberally with the remaining butter, add the raisins to the semolina mixture and put into oven. When a light brown crust is formed, take out, tear with two forks, then return to oven for a few more minutes, until the whole mixture gets a little crisp. Serve hot on a prewarmed plate, sprinkle with sugar and with stewed fruit, preferably stewed plums.

SCHMARREN MADE FROM STALE WHITE BREAD OR ROLLS (Semmelschmarren)

 5 *rolls*   2 *ozs raisins*
 2 *eggs*   2 *ozs butter (4 tablespoons)*
½ *pint milk (1 cup)*

Mix the eggs with the milk, sugar and a tiny pinch of salt, cut the rolls into thin slices and cover with the milk. When the rolls have absorbed the liquid completely, take them out and put them together with the raisins into a fireproof dish in which you have melted the butter and bake until nicely browned.

Now you can make many variations on this simple theme:

1. With cherries added instead of the raisins.

2. Chopped almonds or nuts can be added to the raisins.

3. Peeled and thinly sliced apples are put in layers between the cut rolls, when you put them into the fireproof dish.

4. Grated chocolate can be added generously.

SCHMARREN MADE FROM CROISSANTS (Kipferlschmarren)

Follow the same method, substituing croissants for rolls.

CREAM CHEESE DUMPLINGS (Topfenknödel)

½ *lb semolina (1½ cups)*   2 *ozs breadcrumbs (6 tablespoons)*
½ *lb cream cheese*   2 *ozs butter (4 tablespoons)*
 2 *rolls*

The rolls are cut into small pieces, moistened with a little milk, and then put through the grinder or through a sieve. Add to the cream cheese, then add the semolina, a pinch of salt, the sugar and the eggs. Leave this for an hour. Then make into smallish dumplings and simmer gently in mildly salted boiling water for a quarter of an hour. Fry breadcrumbs golden in the butter, roll the drained dumplings carefully in this and serve with stewed fruit.

RICE PUDDING (Reisauflauf)

3 ozs rice (1 cup)   *2 eggs*
1 pint milk (2 cups)   *grated lemon rind*
1 oz sugar (2 tablespoons)   *1 oz raisins (optional)*
2 ozs butter (4 tablespoons)

Clean the rice and put into boiling milk with a pinch of salt. Cook on a low flame until soft, but not too much so. Remove from heat and leave to cool. Meanwhile, mix the butter with sugar, the egg yolks and the lemon rind; add the rice to this when quite cool (also the raisins when used) now add the stiffly beaten egg whites, and put into a buttered fireproof dish. Bake for three quarters of an hour and serve hot.

You can vary this in the following ways:

1. With apples: prepare as described above putting only half of the rice mixture into dish at first. Now put in a layer of sliced apples and sprinkle with sugar and cinnamon.

Any of the following fruit can be used in the same way, either fresh or frozen: strawberries, raspberries, cherries, pears, apricots, peaches.

2. With jam: any good jam or conserve can be used instead of the fresh fruit, also drained tinned or stewed fruit.

This pudding can be made to look very attractive if you pipe it with beaten egg whites, to which you have added some icing sugar. This can only be done when the pudding is cooked, it must be returned to the oven for a few more minutes, until this meringue mixture is set and slightly browned.

YEAST DUMPLINGS (Germknödel)

One has to be very careful when preparing yeast pastry, and I have given all the necessary do's and don'ts in this chapter. Here, I shall give you the directions also for the Cake Chapter.

For the "Sample"

½ oz yeast	1 teaspoon sugar
½ cup milk	1½ ozs flour (4½ tablespoons)
1 lb flour (4 cups)	1 oz sugar
¼ pint milk (½ cup)	3 ozs butter
2 eggs	pinch of salt

10 ozs Powidl — for Filling   *Explanation of this is to be found at the end of the recipe.*

5 ozs butter (for melting)
1 oz ground poppyseeds   } *This to be served at the table*
1 oz sugar (2 tablespoons)

Crumble the yeast in a cup, then add the milk which should be luke-warm, then add the flour and sugar and mix thoroughly. It should have a consistency similar to that of thick cream. It must now be kept warm, not too hot and not too cold, either can be equally bad; try putting your oven at a low temperature, and then place the cup either above or below where you warm your plates. Leave it there for 15 minutes. If it is in the right temperature it will have risen to the brim of the cup and be quite frothy. Now melt the butter and mix with the eggs, the sugar, the milk (lukewarm) and the flour which should also be warm and slightly salted with the "sample". All ingredients m u s t be warm. I know I've mentioned it before, but one cannot repeat it often enough. The bowl in which you mix it should also be warm. Now mix thoroughly with a large wooden spoon. Beat well, you will see quite clearly when it has been beaten enough, as the dough must come away from both the basin and the cooking spoon easily. Now put the basin into a warm place covered with a clean cloth. If you have no heating on when you prepare this, again the best way is to put it into wherever you warm your plates which should be rather warm, but not hot. Leave it there for 1 hour. After this time, it should have risen to double its former size. Now put some flour on your hands and with the help of a spoon, form a dumpling into the middle of which you put a lump of Powidl. Put the dumpling on a floured pastryboard, and again cover with a cloth; leave for half an hour. If your kitchen is not warm, heat the oven and open the oven door. After half an hour put them into boiling and slightly salted water, but not too many at a time. They should be cooked under cover for three minutes on the one side, then turned round and cooked for four minutes without a lid. They must be taken out at once, pierced with a fork, so that the steam can escape, and then put into a buttered pan into the open heated oven until all the dumplings are cooked. They are served on a warm dish with melted hot butter, ground poppyseeds and sugar.

Don't be frightened to do them, it is really worth a try, and sounds much more complicated than it really is. Perhaps it would be wiser to try your first ones without the filling (called Powidl) which is a very special dry kind of plum jam and which you can make yourself as follows:

POWIDL

Cook some prunes in water until they are quite soft. Take out the stones, now chop them or put them through the mincer, mix with cinnamon, sugar and a little rum on a small flame. Cool.

BAKED MICE (Gebackene Mäuse)

Don't be shocked, this is just another fancy name for a yeast
dessert!

For the "Sample"

1 tablespoon rum	*1 oz sugar (2 tablespoons)*
½ oz yeast	*2 ozs butter (4 tablespoons)*
½ lb flour (2 cups)	*1 oz raisins*
slightly less than ½ pint milk	*1 lb lard or oil for frying*
(1 cup)	*½ pint fruit syrup*

This time the "sample" is made out of the rum and yeast, keep
warm for a quarter of an hour. In a warm basin now mix with the
salted slightly warmed flour, the lukewarm milk, sugar, egg yolks,
the melted butter and beat well with a wooden spoon, until the
mixture comes away from the spoon, add the raisins and put into a
warm place for an hour. Then put the fat into a large deep frying
pan. Heat it until it is piping hot, dip a tablespoon into this and
form shapes the size of the spoon, dropping them into the hot fat.
Shake pan a little, then fry slowly. Take out, let them drain off on
some filter paper. Serve hot with raspberry syrup.

STEAMNOODLES WITH VANILLA CREAM
(Dampfnudeln mit Crème)

They are called Noodles — but don't be fooled — they're really
more of an oblong dumpling.

6 ozs flour (1½ cups)	*1½ ozs butter*
⅓ oz yeast	*2 egg yolks*
⅙ pint milk	*1½ ozs sugar (4½ tablespoons)*

For the pan: *2 ozs butter (4 tablespoons) and ⅛ pint milk.*

For the vanilla cream:

¼ pint milk	*½ oz cornflour*
3 ozs sugar	*1 vanillapod*
2 egg yolks	

Make a "Sample" in the usual way. Crumble the yeast in a cup
with 1 tablespoonful of the milk, a pinch of sugar and as much
flour until you get a thick cream consistency. Put cup in a warm
place for 15 minutes. Now melt the butter with the egg yolks, the

lukewarm milk, the sugar, the "sample", a pinch of salt and the warmed flour. Stir this batter which should by now be fairly soft. Now beat with a wooden spoon until it comes away from the spoon. Sprinkle with a little flour, put into a warm place covered with a cloth and leave for an hour. Now take your pastryboard, flour it a little, form a roll about 1 inch thick. Cut into pieces about 2 inches long and dip into the butter (the 2 ozs which you have melted) and place them side by side in a pan into which you have poured the milk — it should be about ½ inch deep. Now cover with a cloth and leave for another half hour in the warm kitchen so that they can rise a little more. Meanwhile, heat the oven, and after you have brushed the top of the risen noodles with some more melted butter, bake until golden on top. Serve hot with Vanilla sauce.

For the Vanilla cream: into a double boiler put the milk, the vanilla pod, the sugar and the cornflour. Beat over boiling water until it has become quite thick. Then remove from heat and beat for 5 more minutes. Take the vanilla pod out and serve.

MILK AND CREAM STRUDEL (Millirahmstrudel)

Strudelteig (See under Pastries)
2 rolls
¼ pint sour cream (½ cup)
3 ozs sugar (½ cup)
5 oz butter (¾ cup)
1 oz butter (2 tablespoons) for brushing, and the baking dish

1 tablespoon lemon juice
grated rind of ½ lemon
2 eggs
1 oz raisins
½ pint milk

Canarymilk

1 egg yolk
½ pint milk (1 cup)
1½ ozs sugar (¼ cup)
1 vanilla pod

Prepare the strudelpastry as described, spread on a slightly damp cloth and spread with the following filling: Cream the butter with the sugar, the eggyolks, the lemon rind, lemon juice, and the two rolls which you have soaked in a little milk and water and put through the mincer or sieve after having squeezed them well. Lastly, add the washed and cleaned raisins, gradually the sour cream and then the stiffly beaten egg whites. Mix well and spread the Strudel evenly. Now roll together with the cloth, by lifting the cloth at one end and rolling away from it as with a Swiss roll. Butter a fireproof dish, and lift the strudel carefully into this by rolling it up like a snail. Now brush with melted butter and put into heated oven. When the strudel is slightly browned, pour the boiling milk over it and bake for 10 more minutes in the hot oven. Serve with hot "Canary milk": beat the egg yolk in a double boiler with the milk, the sugar and the vanilla pod until quite foamy.

CHEESE STRUDEL (Topfenstrudel)

Strudelteig (See under Pastries)	¼ *pint sour cream*
3 ozs butter (6 tablespoons)	*grated lemon rind*
2½ ozs sugar (6 tablespoons)	*1 oz raisins*
2 eggs	½ *pint milk (1 cup)*
¾ *lb cream cheese*	*butter for the dish*

Prepare the strudel in the described method and when spread on a cloth, fill with the following: cream the butter with the sugar, the egg yolks, the lemon rind, the cream and the creamcheese and finally the beaten egg whites. Roll up and put into a buttered fireproof dish as described in previous recipe and bake until golden brown. Now pour boiling milk over and leave for ten more minutes in hot oven. Serve hot with Canary milk.

N o t e : This strudel can also be eaten cold, in which case it has to be brushed with melted butter before being put into the oven, no milk is added. The strudel is sprinkled with vanilla sugar when it is baked golden brown, and the Canary milk is omitted.

The recipes which I have given you so far are more of the "everyday" type, and you will find them under the Menus for everyday use at the end of the book. But now let's go into the field of our more "elegant" warm desserts:

First and foremost, the famous —

146

SALZBURGER NOCKERL

3 ozs butter for the dish (6 table-   5 egg whites
   spoons)   1 tablespoon of flour
4 egg yolks

It is not as difficult as you may think! Just work carefully and lightly. The best thing is to heat the oven before you begin. Then separate the egg whites and beat them very stiffly, this is the most important part - that the whites are r e a l l y stiff. A flat fire-proof dish is put on a small flame and is heated gradually. When you have beaten the egg whites, put the butter into this dish and let it melt. Now stir in the egg yolks (in this case the yolks are stirred into the white and not the other way round) with the flour, gently, carefully, and form three large 'blobs' in the foaming butter — these 'blobs' should be rather pointed. Over a medium flame the bottom of the 'blobs' (Nockerl) should just set. This will take about 1 minute, then very quickly, as fast as possible, put the dish into the heated oven. Leave there until the tops are nicely browned, this only takes two or three minutes. Then take out, dust with icing sugar and serve at once.

SOUFFLÉ

I am giving you the basic recipe which can be varied by adding 2 ozs of plain chocolate, or 3 ozs of any jam.

3 ozs icing sugar (³/₄ cup)   *7 egg whites*
butter for the dish

Cream three of the egg whites with the sugar and either the jam or chocolate, until quite stiff. Now add the stiffly beaten remaining 4 egg whites. Pour into buttered soufflé dish and bake for 15 minutes in moderately hot oven. Serve at once.

STRAWBERRY SOUFFLÉ (Erdbeer-Omelette)

Is made in the same way as the above, only a few fresh strawberries are sliced and added to the omelette mixture. For the filling, crushed strawberries are used. Almost all berries can be used, but take care only to add a very few to the omelette mixture - it must not be too heavy.

CHOCOLATE SOUFFLÉ (Schokolade-Omelette)

Is made in the same way as the "Stephanie" but add two tablespoons of finely grated plain chocolate and serve chocolate sauce instead of a filling with it. For the Chocolate sauce: melt a few bars of plain chocolate to which are added a few drops of boiling water.

LEMON SOUFFLÉ (Zitronen-Omelette)

6 eggs   *1 tablespoon butter*
3 ozs sugar (³/₄ cup)   *1 tablespoon biscuit crumbs*
1 lemon

Grate the lemon rind from the lemon, squeeze out the juice, separate the egg whites, beat them stiffly, adding the sugar. Mix the egg yolks with the lemon rind and the crumbs, adding the lemon juice. Lastly, fold in the egg whites. Heat the butter in an omelette pan, spread well, pour the mixture in and bake slowly in a heated oven. Serve at once.

CHOCOLATE PUDDING WITH CHOCOLATE SAUCE & WHIPPED CREAM, CALLED "MOOR IN HIS SHIRT"
(Mohr im Hemd)

5 eggs
2½ ozs butter (⅓ cup)
3 ozs sugar
2½ ozs almonds
3 ozs chocolate

Chocolate sauce:

3 ozs plain chocolate
3 ozs sugar (6 tablespoons)
1 knob butter
1 cup water

Cream the butter with the sugar and the egg yolks, then add the melted chocolate, the peeled and ground almonds and two tablespoons of fine breadcrumbs or spongecake crumbs and the stiffly beaten egg whites. Butter a pudding basin and sprinkle it with sugar. Now fill in with the pudding mixture (the basin should only be ¾ full). Cover and cook for one hour. For the Chocolate sauce: in a double boiler, mix the sugar with the melted chocolate and the butter until thick, then add the butter and pour over the pudding when this is cooked. Serve whipped cream separately. It can be eaten cold.

WINE PUDDING

4 ozs sugar (½ cup and 1 tablespoon)
7 eggs
4 ozs spongecake crumbs
2 ozs butter (4 tablespoons)
the chopped peel of half a lemon
¼ pint white wine

Chaudeau:

½ pint white wine (1 cup)
 4 ozs sugar (½ cup and 1 tablespoon)
three egg yolks

149

Whisk the sugar, the egg yolks and the finely cut lemon peel until quite foamy, add the spongecake crumbs, the stiffly whipped egg whites, and the melted butter. Now pour into a greased and floured pudding form, cover and cook for half an hour. Now pour the wine over it and cook for another half hour. Serve hot with the following sauce:

C h a u d e a u : Put the wine, the egg yolks and the sugar with the wine into a double boiler and beat until quite thick, keep hot by letting it stand in the double boiler.

STEPHANIE-OMELETTE

3 eggs
2 tablespoons butter
2 tablespoons flour
3 tablespoons cream

2 tablespoons icing sugar
jam, crushed fresh, or drained tinned or frozen fruit for filling

Beat the egg whites stiffly. Fold in the egg yolks, the sugar and the cream, add the flour carefully. In an ovenproof omelette pan you have meanwhile heated the butter, turn the pan around so that the butter is spread evenly. Put the mixture into the pan and into a fairly hot oven. It should remain there for about 15 minutes. Slip onto heated serving dish, and put the filling into one side and fold over the other (the filling should have at least room temperature, and so if you use jam it should also be heated). Serve at once.

Desserts (cold)

STUFFED ORANGES (Gefüllte Orangen)

Take 5 large oranges, cut them in half — making 10 shells. Squeeze out all juice, taking care to keep the shells intact. You should obtain about ½ pint of orange juice from this quantity of oranges. To this, add then six egg yolks and 7 ozs (1 cup and 1 tablespoon) of sugar. Put into a doubleboiler and whisk over flame until thick. Take off flame and add 1 oz of gelatine (mixed with a little water beforehand), whisk well. When cool, add ¼ pint (½ cup) of whipped cream and fill into orangeshells. Chill well before serving.

150

SNOW-NOCKERL MADE FROM EGG WHITES (Schneenockerln)

6 whites of egg   6 tablespoons icing sugar

Vanilla sauce: 6 egg yolks
1½ pints milk (3 cups)   4 - 5 tablespoons sugar
1 tablespoon cornflour   1 vanilla pod

Whisk the eggs stiffly, gradually adding the icing sugar. In a large shallow saucepan bring the milk to the boil with one vanilla pod. When it starts to rise put in the Nockerl with a large table or serving spoon. Lower the heat and be careful that the Nockerl do not touch. Simmer for three minutes, then turn over with a palette knife and simmer for another three minutes. Lift the Nockerl out with a perforated spoon and place them on a shallow serving bowl. Use up the remaining egg white mixture in the same way. Now mix the egg yolks in a bowl with the cornflour and the sugar and four tablespoons of milk. Measure the milk in which you have cooked the Nockerl, it should be 1¼ pints (2½ cups), mix with the yolks, and cornflour mixture, put into doubleboiler and cook, stirring continuously until thick. Pour over the Nockerl, chill well before serving. Remove vanilla pod.

Fresh strawberries or raspberries can be arranged on top if liked, and if you want to simplify this dish, use your favorite vanilla pudding mixture instead of the recipe I've given you, but use a little more milk than usual, the crème should be liquid.

KLOSTERSCHWESTERN

(Literally translated this of course means "Nuns" — the reason? I wouldn't know, but somehow it makes it more interesting to have a name like this!)

Take one large pear for each person (either fresh or bottled), fresh ones are peeled, halved and stewed with a little sugar — take care that they don't get too soft. Drain off the liquid and arrange the pears one on top of the other in a glass dish. The chocolate sauce is then poured over them. The method for this is as follows: melt bars of good plain chocolate, gradually stirring in a few drops of boiling water, till you have the right consistency for a thick chocolate sauce, don't add sugar! Chill well. Before serving, cover with sweetened whipped cream. It tastes delicious and is so easy and quick to make.

COLD RICE WITH FRUIT (Kalter Reis mit Obst)

1 cup rice
2 pints (4 cups) milk
3/4 pint of whipping cream
* (1 1/2 cups)*

2 ozs sugar (1/2 cup)
diced tinned, fresh or candied fruit

Wash and dry the rice and cook until soft in boiling milk, to which you have added the sugar and one vanilla pod. Leave to cool. Whip the cream until quite stiff and fold into the cold rice. A pudding form or a rice ring is brushed very lightly with fine tasteless oil. Now put in a layer of rice, some diced tinned fruit which you have drained well, or fresh strawberries or raspberries. Continue with another layer of rice, and so on. Put in the ice-box for at least five hours, it must be thoroughly chilled. Turn out (you'll find it easier if you put a damp hot cloth on top of the form for a few seconds), and serve with fruit syrup (again raspberry or strawberry is best) and some more whipped cream. The fruit inside is optional, it also tastes very good with fruit syrup only.

Now I'll give you a basic recipe for C r ê m e that can be varied in many ways and can be served either in individual glasses or in a glass fruit bowl — and can be decorated further for festive occasions.

1 pint milk (2 cups)
5 ozs sugar (3/4 cup)
8 leaves of gelatine or 1/2 oz powde-
* red gelatine (1 1/2 bare tablespoons)*

1 oz cornflour (1/4 cup)
1 pint cream (2 cups)
6 egg yolks

Dissolve the gelatine in a little cold water. Mix the milk, the sugar, the yolks and the cornflour thoroughly and bring to the boil in a double boiler stirring constantly. Add the gelatine and while stirring, take away from the burner. Now beat well until quite cool. Whip the cream and add ¾ of it to the Crème, the rest is used for piping or other decoration. Chill well. You can add the various flavours to this, but do so before adding the whipped cream. Here are a few suggestions for flavouring:

C o f f e e: add powdered coffee or strong black coffee, decorate with roasted almonds.

C h o c o l a t e: add melted plain chocolate, decorate with chocolate shavings.

S t r a w b e r r i e s: add fresh crushed ones, decorate with whole strawberries and green candied peel.

O r a n g e: add orange syrup and orange slices, decorate with orange wedges.

H a z e l n u t s o r A l m o n d s: add ground roasted nuts, decorate with chopped nuts.

Raspberries, Pineapple, Redcurrants, Bananas, Lemons, can be used in the same way as strawberries. You can also fill the Crème into slightly oiled forms and turn it out.

WITCHES FOAM (Hexenschaum)

3 medium cooking apples
2 tablespoons apricot jam
1 tablespoon lemon juice
3 ozs sugar (¾ cup)
1 teaspoon rum or maraschino
4 egg whites

Bake the apples until they are soft, put through a sieve.
Whisk the egg whites, gradually adding the sugar, the jam, the apple purée, the rum and the lemon juice. Continue whisking until it is quite stiff. Chill well before serving.

153

FRUIT CREME (Früchtencrême)

6 egg yolks
3 ozs (slightly less than ½ cup)
  sugar
1 bare tablespoon cornflour

3 gelatine leaves or 1 tablespoon
  powdered gelatine
1 vanilla pod
1 pint (2 cups) milk
½ pint whipped cream

And some spongecake, some tinned apricots, peaches and or cherries (Chocolate cake can also be used) — this is an excellent way to use up left-over cake.

In a doubleboiler whisk the egg yolks, the sugar, the cornflour, the vanilla pod and the milk to a thick crême. Beat until cool, then add the gelatine (dissolved in a little water) the stiffly whipped cream and the spongecake cut into cubes. Rinse a mould with cold water, put in some of the crême alternatively with the drained fruit until everything is used up. Put into the ice or the deepfreezer - everything must be quite set (or in the deep freeze it will have turned to ice cream). Turn out onto flat plate (if it does not come out easily, press a hot damp cloth for a few minutes over the mould). Garnish with candied fruit and pipe with whipped cream.

SUMMER CREME (Obst mit saurem Rahm)

A delicious and simple Summer sweeet is F r u i t a n d S o u r C r e a m or Yoghourt. This is something you will not find in restaurants, but which is eaten in most Austrian homes.

To a pint of sour cream (those who want to slim, can use yoghourt or thick sour milk) allow 1 pound of strawberries, raspberries or blueberries (one or the other). Put half of the fruit into a bowl, crush with three tablespoons of sugar, pour the cream on top, mix well. Now add the rest of the fruit (whole in the case of raspberries and blueberries, strawberries should be halved). Chill well before serving.

CREME BELVEDERE

5 ozs plain chocolate	*5 ozs butter*
5 eggs	*3 tablespoons sugar*

Melt the chocolate with three tablespoons of boiling water, add the sugar and the 5 egg yolks, stir until a completely smooth crême is obtained. Now add the stiffly whisked 5 egg whites to this and put into a savarin, rice ring, or a pudding mould which should not be too deep, and which should be rinsed in cold water. Put in boiling water, be careful that no water can get into it until it is set. Leave to cool, then put in the icebox. Turn out and pipe with whipped cream.

Small Pastries and Cakes

Now that we have come to baking, I should tell you that we hardly use any prefabricated cake mixtures. You may think us very much behind the times, and in a way you may be right, but let me explain our outlook on this. We still like to do the preliminary preparations ourselves. We find pleasure in weighing the ingredients, kneading the dough and filling the whole kitchen with a delightful aroma which comes only with the preparation of a cake. Of course it takes longer than using a cake mixture, but this shouldn't really put you off. On the other hand, don't let me put you off using cake mixtures — go on using them by all means — they must be very good judging from the way they look in the advertisements!

I would even suggest that you try speedier versions of our cakes and pastries by substituting those cake mixes which produce exactly or near enough the type of base which I describe. You can try sponge mixtures, yeast mixtures, chocolate cake mixture; I believe you can also buy ready made Strudel and puff pastry, but by all means use the fillings and crême that I give you — or there won't be anything Austrian left! If you can get prefabricated icing, use this too, but it should be flavourless and plain, to which you add your own coffee, chocolate or other flavouring. But now that I've made this concession, you must promise me that you'll follow the original recipes without the substitutes when you do have some spare time — it isn't really the same unless you do.

PROFITEROLES — ECLAIRS — (Brandteigkrapferln)

3 ozs butter
5 ozs flour
5 ozs milk
6 eggs

I c i n g:
6 ozs chocolate
3 ozs butter

Put the butter and milk into a saucepan. Bring quickly to the boil, then lower the flame and add the flour. On a very low flame mix with a wooden spoon until a very firm and fat pastry has formed, to which you add the eggs, after you have taken off the flame. It is best to put the pastry now into a different basin and add one egg after the other, stirring and mixing thoroughly after each egg. Now leave this for about one hour, it should be quite cool before you start to bake. Grease the baking sheet slightly, dip two teaspoons into a cup of white of egg, and with these two spoons form little shapes in the size of a walnut, which you drop onto the baking sheet. Always dip the spoons into the egg white and leave enough space for the little puffs to rise. Put into a hot oven and leave there for 25 minutes. Don't open the oven before that time. The puffs should have risen and must be slit open on one side. Inside they should be quite hollow. When cool they are filled with slightly sweetened whipped cream, and covered with the following icing: Melt the chocolate in a double boiler, add the butter, stir until smooth and let cool slightly, then pour about a tablespoon over each filled puff.

The Krapferl can also be filled with the following:

1. Whipped cream, to which a little strawberry or raspberry jam has been added for colouring, and some whole or halves of either of these berries. Ice with pink icing.

157

2. With whipped cream to which a little grated chocolate has been added.

3. With whipped cream to which a spoonful of powdered coffee has been added. Ice with coffee icing (see under NUSSROULADE). Pink icing is the same, a little pink food colouring being added instead of the coffee.

MERINGUES (Windbäckerei)

This is an excellent way of using up egg whites, but they must be quite fresh. Allow 5 - 6 tablespoons of granulated sugar to one egg white (it depends on the size of the egg). In this particular case, the oven temperature is very important, and the best way to describe this is to say that when a piece of white paper yellows quickly without burning, then it is right.

Take 6 egg whites and the relevant quantity of sugar. Beat the whites stiffly, then add a third of your sugar quantity, spoon by spoon, beating all the time. When the mixture is quite stiff, add the rest of the sugar, stirring lightly.

On a buttered and floured baking sheet, form little heaps or pipe to any shape you want. Put into the cool oven where it is left for 1½ to 2 hours. It should rise a little and then colour to a slight yellow. Keep the temperature even all the time. Take off the sheet while still warm.

COFFEE MERINGUES

Powdered coffee is added to the egg and sugar mixture, so that you obtain a light coffee colour. Again small clusters of the mixture are formed and treated the same way as in the first recipe. It is delicious when served with a crême consisting of stiffly whipped cream to which a little icing sugar and some powdered coffee have been added. Put this in a glass bowl and decorate with walnuts and drained and stoned stewed prunes, which you cut into small pieces. Serve the meringues separately on a flat plate.

MOZARTKUGELN

These are delicious sweets which you normally buy at the Confectioner's, and are more of a "Candy".

1st mixture:
5 ozs (1 cup) grated almonds
5 ozs (not quite 1 cup) icing
   sugar
1 teaspoon white of egg

Coating:
3 ozs plain chocolate
1 piece of butter (the size of a
   walnut)

2nd mixture:
6 ozs (1 cup) icing sugar
4 ozs (3/4 cup) ground walnuts
2 ozs plain chocolate
1 white of egg
1 teaspoon rum

Skin and oven-dry the almonds and grate them as finely as possible. Now mix into paste with the egg white and the sugar, if liked add a little green colouring to this. Form into small balls the size of a small marble. Prepare the 2nd mixture: Grate the walnuts, add the sugar, the rum, the egg white and lastly, the chocolate, which you have melted in the oven. Form this into a paste also, and shape over the first little ball. This is done by taking enough

159

of the chocolate mixture into the palm of your hand, then put the first ball on top and coat around it, the covering should be about a quarter of an inch thick all over. For the chocolate coating: melt the chocolate, adding two tablespoons of boiling water and the butter, insert the balls one by one, coating them well and take them out carefully with the tips of two forks. Put on wire rack overnight to dry, and then put in white paper caps.

NUT DESSERT (Nußkugerln)

6 ozs walnuts
6 ozs (not quite 1 cup) sugar
1½ ozs mixed candied fruit and
 peel

2 egg whites
nuts for decoration
chocolate covering (see under
 Mozartkugeln)

Chop the candied fruit, and put into a basin. Add the ground walnuts the sugar and the egg whites. Mix well and form into small balls, the size of a walnut. Cover with chocolate icing (see under Mozartkugerln) and put one half walnut on top, then cool and arrange in paper capsules.

VANILLA CRESCENTS (Vanillekipferln)

2½ ozs grated almonds (½ cup)
5 ozs sugar (¾ cup)
Vanilla sugar for coating.

7½ ozs (1 cup) butter
10 ozs (2½ cups) flour

Grind the unpeeled almonds. Sift the flour, add the sugar and almonds. Now cut the butter into small pieces and crumbling it, mix well with the dry ingredients. Knead well on a pastryboard. Now take a piece of the paste and roll into a long roll the thickness of your thumb. Cut this into even pieces about 2 to 2½ inches long. Form them into small crescents (the ends should be a little shaped!) put onto a buttered and floured baking sheet and bake in medium hot oven until golden brown. While still hot put into a bowl with vanilla icing sugar (see Essentials) coat the crescents completely (be careful, they break easily!). Take out and leave until cool. They can be kept in a tin for quite some time, and actually improve with keeping.

TARTLETS FROM ISCHL (Ischler Törtchen)

Ischl is a delightful small town in Upper Austria, on the borders of the famous Salzkammergut. It is best known for the fact that the Emperor Franz Joseph spent his holidays there, he even met his Empress Elisabeth there for the first time, and so it became the summer resort of all society of the Austro-Hungarian Monarchy. Part of that ancient glory still reaches us, for when you sit at Zauner's, the famous Konditorei there, you feel it might be possible without too much exertion of the imagination to transport yourself back to that very colourful period.

6 ozs (1½ cups) sifted flour   3 ozs (½ cup) sugar
6 ozs (⁴/₅ cup) butter   3¾ ozs (¾ cup) ground almonds
Apricot or redcurrant jam

On a pastry board mix the sifted flour with the skinned, dried and ground almonds and the sugar, crumble the butter well into this, knead thoroughly, shape into a ball and leave on the board for about an hour Now roll with rolling pin to ⅛ inch thickness, then cut into rounds with pastry cutter or tumbler measuring 2½ to 3 inches across. Bake in medium oven on a buttered and floured baking sheet. When cold, spread with heated jam, put two together as with a sandwich and coat with chocolate icing.

EQUAL WEIGHT CAKE WITH FRUIT
(Gleichgewichtskuchen mit Obst)

Take the weight of 4 eggs for butter

Take the weight of 4 eggs for sugar

Take the weight of 4 eggs for flour

and than 4 eggs also of course

Cream the butter and the sugar, add the egg yolks and the flour to which you have added a pinch of baking powder, lastly add the stiffly beaten egg whites. Put on a buttered baking sheet, cover with any fruit in season. Apricots and plums or peaches should be sliced. (Berries are not used for this cake.)

BLACK CHERRY CAKE (Schwarzer Kirschenkuchen)

Take the weight of 4 eggs for: Sugar, butter, unskinned almonds,

ground chocolate

and than 4 eggs also of course

Separate the eggs. Cream the butter with the sugar, add the egg yolks, the ground almonds and lastly the stiffly beaten egg whites. Put on a buttered and floured baking sheet, one with a rim, cover with cherries (preferably morella) about an inch apart. Bake slowly in a medium oven.

DATE KISSES (Dattelbusserln)

3½ ozs (²/₃ cup) almonds
7 ozs sugar (1 cup and 1 table-spoons)

3 egg whites
3 ozs dates

Cut the dates into small thin strips, skin, dry and cut the almonds into thin strips, beat the egg whites stiffly with one third of the sugar. Now fold in the remaining sugar, the dates and the almonds. With the help of a spoon and a fork, drop in small heaps on small rounds of rice paper. Bake in a moderate oven.

ANGELS' KISSES (Engelsbusserln)

I think I must explain what a "Busserl" is! It is Viennese dialect for a kiss — and I should also add that a "Busserl" is always of the small, harmless variety! The kiss a child gives to his mother, the careless one exchanged in the Fasching (carnival), a sign of affection shown to a dear friend either sex. It might of course lead to more, but at the beginning, it is something very Austrian, gay, friendly, light... something like these delicious little pastries which have derived their name from it:

3½ ozs (²/₃ cup) almonds   a little more than 2 ozs (¹/₃ cup)
1 egg white   sugar
1 teaspoon lemon juice   1 teaspoon grated lemon rind

Skin, dry and grate the almonds; beat the egg white, fold in the almonds, the lemon rind, sugar and the lemon juice. Form into walnut sized shapes which you place on small rounds of rice paper. Bake in cool oven until slightly coloured.

WIDOWS' KISSES (Witwenküsse)

5 ozs chopped nuts   4 egg whites
5 ozs (³/₄ cup) sugar   5 ozs chopped, mixed candied peel

In a double boiler whisk egg whites and sugar until it becomes thick over the steam. Remove from burner and whisk until cool, now fold in the coarsely chopped walnuts and the finely chopped peel. Arrange on small rounds of rice paper and bake in moderate oven until slightly coloured.

JAM CRESCENTS (Alt-Wiener Kipferln)

½ lb almonds
¼ cup sugar

2 tablespoons apricot, raspberry or
redcurrant jam

It is difficult to give the exact amount of jam as this depends on its consistency. Put the unskinned almonds through the grinder, add the sugar and as much jam as the mixture will take, so that you can form small crescents. Put on a buttered baking sheet into a cool oven, they should d r y rather than bake. It is best to try one first and then adjust the mixture with more jam.

GRANDMOTHER'S BUNS (Großmutters Krapferln)
(I think they have another name, but in our family this is how they were always called.)

5 ozs walnuts
5 ozs (¾ cup) sugar
2 egg whites

3 egg whites
1 heaped tablespoon flour
¼ cup icing sugar

Stir the 2 egg whites with the ground nuts for 20 minutes.
Now whisk 3 egg whites stiffly, to this add 1 heaped tablespoon of flour and ¼ cup of icing sugar. Stir this gently into the first mixture. Pipe little buns on a baking sheet onto which you have put a moistened sheet of paper, sprinkle with sugar and bake in a very moderate oven until a light crust has formed. When the little buns are cool, put two together with the following crême: 2 ozs butter, 1 melted bar of plain chocolate, 1 egg, 2 ozs sugar, 2 ozs ground walnuts.

HEDGEHOGS (Igel)

Are made in the same way as meringues, fairly large heaps are formed, and into these, very thin slices of blanched almonds are inserted to make the spikes of the hedgehog. Serve whipped cream separately.

HUSSAR'S BUNS (Husarenkrapferl)

1 oz almonds (for sprinkling)   *aprox. 2 ozs apricot jam*
4 ozs (1 cup) flour   *2¼ ozs (¹/₃ cup) butter*
1 egg yolk and one egg white   *a little more than 3 ozs sugar*

On a pastry board mix the sifted flour with the sugar, the egg yolk and the crumbled butter, when kneaded well leave for an hour or chill in ice-box for half an hour. Form into small balls between your hands (about the size of a walnut). Place these balls on a buttered and floured baking sheet, dip the end of a wooden cooking spoon into flour and make small holes in the middle of each ball. Brush with egg white and sprinkle with the almonds which you have blanched and chopped. Bake in medium oven until golden, remove from sheet while still warm, put on wire rack and insert a dash of apricot jam into each hole, which will have shrunk a little during the baking. Dust with vanilla icing sugar.

STRUDELPASTRY

This is the basis of the famous Viennese Apfelstrudel, for which I shall give you the simplest method. There are recipes which use an egg, white of egg or yolk of egg as well, but this is not essential. Melted butter can be used instead of oil. Strudel can also be made of yeast paste or Butterteig (puff pastry) but the real Viennese Apfelstrudel is always as follows:

8 ozs (2 cups) flour   *¼ oz (1 teaspoon) oil — or 1 teas-*
½ cup (¼ pint) warm water   *poon butter*

On the pastry board we put the sieved flour with a pinch of salt in the shape of a small mound. Make a dent in the middle which will hold the oil. Mix well and add the warm water, then knead well. The paste is ready when it comes away from your hands easily. Now form into a ball, brush lightly with a little oil or dust with flour and cover with a bowl. It should remain under this bowl, which should be prewarmed, in a warm place for ¾ of an hour. Meanwhile you can prepare the filling. After half an hour's pause, the dough is ready for "pulling". Spread your kitchen table with a clean tablecloth, dust this lightly with flour. Place the dough on the cloth (use your largest table or halve the dough) and roll out carefully with rolling pin as far as it will go. Brush with a little oil, slip your hands underneath the dough and start pulling gently with the back of your hands first, then with your thumbs, rather than your fingers. Do this gently and carefully .Don't worry if it tears, it does take a lot of practise! Pull out to paper thinness. The ends which always remain too thick, must be cut off, they can be cut and used for soup. When the dough is quite thin, brush with oil or melted butter; leave on the cloth for ten minutes then fill it.

APPLE STRUDEL (Apfelstrudel)

½ cup raisins
1 cup sugar
⅓ cup butter (for frying bread-
    crumbs
2 tablespoons butter (for brush-
    ing the pastry)

pinch cinnamon
1½ lbs apple
2 cups breadcrumbs

Fry the breadcrumbs golden brown in the butter, leave to cool. Peel the apples and slice them as small and as thinly as possible into a bowl, add the sugar, a pinch of cinnamon and the cleaned raisins. Onto the Strudelpastry now spread the breadcrumbs and to one half the apple mixture. Roll the Strudel by lifting the cloth on the side where the apple mixture has been spread. Roll carefully as a swiss roll and then place on a buttered baking sheet. Close the ends by pinching them together. Brush with half of the melted butter and put into a moderately hot oven for about three quarters of an hour. During the baking, brush once more with melted butter. Serve hot or cold and sprinkle with vanilla sugar while still hot.

CHERRY STRUDEL (Kirschenstrudel)

Is prepared the same way but the raisins are omitted and the apples are replaced by the equivalent weight of cherries.

RHUBARB STRUDEL

Again the same method and no raisins, 1½ lbs of rhubarb cut into 2 inch pieces is used. This tastes excellent, but might need a little more sugar.

Apricots, plums, grapes are less frequently used, but are also tasty.

CHEESE STRUDEL (Topfenstrudel) ⎫
CREAM STRUDEL (Millirahmstrudel) ⎬ see under warm Desserts

YEAST PASTRIES AND CAKES

For the preparation of the pastry, see under Warm Desserts.

POPPYSEED STRUDEL (Mohnstrudel)

¼ *pint (½ cup) milk*
2 *ozs (¼ cup and 1 tablespoon)*
3 *ozs (⅓ cup and 1 tablespoon)*

Sample:

1 *oz yeast*
⅛ *pint milk*
1 *oz (¼ cup) flour*
1 *scant tablespoon sugar*

Filling:

6 *ozs ground poppyseeds*
slightly less than 1 cup milk
grated lemon peel
not quite 2 ozs butter (¼ cup)
1 *egg for brushing the Strudel*
3 *ozs sugar (¾ cup)*
2 *tablespoons raisins*
pinch cinnamon

Prepare the dough as described. After is has risen, put on a floured pastryboard and knead carefully, until it is quite smooth, then roll out gently to about one tenth of an inch (about the thickness of the back of a knife). Spread with filling, roll up like a Swiss roll, put onto a buttered and floured baking sheet, if it is too large (which it nearly always is) shape like a horseshoe. You can also insert the whole Strudel into a buttered and floured Guglhupf form (fluted cake mould), if you have one. Cover with a cloth and leave for half hour in a warm place so that it can rise. Now brush with the egg (which you have whisked well), and put into warm oven.

Filling: Cook the poppy seeds in the milk, when thick, take off burner and stir in the butter, sugar, the lemon rind, cinnamon and raisins. Cool before using.

YEAST STRUDEL WITH WALNUT FILLING (Nußstrudel)

Is prepared the same way as the Poppyseed strudel. This time the filling consists of:

5 ozs (1½ cups) sugar	1 oz butter
10 ozs ground walnuts	1 tablespoon rum

Bring the sugar with ½ cup of milk to the boil, take off burner, mix to this the butter, the ground nuts and the rum, leave to cool. When quite cold, spread on Strudel as in above recipe.

The strudel can also be spread with jam, or sprinkled with cinnamon and sugar. All these fillings can be filled into Buchteln (small yeastcakes) the preparation of which you will find under "Dampfnudeln" in "Hot Desserts".

PLAITED LOAF (Striezel)

Out of the yeastcake mixture, a plaited loaf can also be made. Simply part the pastry into three parts and on the floured pastry board plait and stick the ends together. Brush with egg and sprinkle with coarsely chopped blanched almonds. Raisins and grated lemon peel can be added to the dough. Bake for 30 - 40 minutes.

YEAST GUGLHUPF (Germguglhupf)

Prepare the pastry as usual, only this time use ¾ pint of milk and add ½ cup of raisins, then let the mixture rise. Butter and flour a Guglhupf mould (preferably the fluted kind, but an ordinary round one can also be used) and put some skinned and halved almonds in the flutes; insert the paste, let it rise again, then bake in medium hot oven. Turn out and sprinkle liberally with vanilla icing sugar.

YEASTGUGLHUPF WITH RUM (Germguglhupf mit Rum)

Prepare as the above, omitting the raisins and almonds. When Guglhupf is baked, turn onto a warmed dish and pour over the following sauce: ½ pint of water is brought to the boil with the grated yellow peel of half a lemon and 6 ozs (1½ cups) sugar, add ¼ pint of rum and the juice of the half lemon. Pour hot over Guglhupf.

GUGLHUPF WITH ORANGE SAUCE

Is the same as above with a different sauce: ½ cup of water and 1½ cups of sugar are brought to the boil (take care not to let it get too brown as there is very little liquid), add the juice of two oranges and the finely grated peel of one orange.

169

APPLE CAKE MADE FROM YEAST (Apfelkuchen aus Germteig)

Prepare the pastry as described in Hot Desserts. Grease a baking sheet and put the paste onto this spreading it gently with your floured hands. On to this, spread thinly sliced peeled apples, sprinkle with sugar and let the whole thing rise, then bake in medium hot oven.

CHERRY CAKE is prepared in the same way, also:

PLUM CAKE (the fruit is stoned and halved).

APRICOT CAKE (the fruit is stoned and halved).

PEACH CAKE (the fruit is stoned and halved).

BLUEBERRY CAKE is spread with blueberries which can be sprinkled with ground gingerbread and sugar (before baking).

CHOCOLATE TIN LOAF (Rehrücken)

This is a Chocolate cake baked in a specially shaped cake tin resembling a saddle of venison. It is fluted, and has an indentation down the middle. But of course you can also bake it in an ordinary cake tin. If you bake it in the traditional Rehrücken form, ice it with chocolate icing and stick in strips of blanched almonds all over, to give the impression of bacon strips which are put into real venison. If you use an ordinary long narrow slab cake tin, you can also do this, and put a line of redcurrant jelly or cranberry jelly down the middle.

5 ozs butter (½ cup plus 3 tablespoons)
6 ozs sugar (⅘ cup)
8 eggs
6 ozs almonds
4 ozs chocolate
2 ozs spongecake crumbs

For cholate icing see under Sachertorte
1 oz blanched almonds for decoration
redcurrant or cranberry jelly

Melt the chocolate, and cream with the butter and the sugar, add the egg yolks one after the other and when all eight have been

170

added, stir for half an hour! Now whisk the egg whites, add the spongecakes crumbs and the unskinned ground almonds to this. Stir the second mixture carefully into the first. Put into a buttered and floured cake tin and bake slowly in a medium oven. When cool, ice and decorate as described above. Serve whipped cream separately.

PASTRY CAKES WITH FRUIT (Obsttörtchen)

5 ozs flour (1¼ cups)   1 oz sugar (3 tablespoons)
6½ ozs butter (½ plus ⅓ cup)   2 egg yolks
milk or cream (as much as the paste will take).
Compôte, canned or fresh fruit (should be strained as dry as possible).

On a pastryboard, mix the butter with the flour, the sugar and the egg yolks, add as much cream or milk to get a smooth consistency, then shape into a lump and put in the icebox for an hour. Butter small pastrycases, roll out the pastry to the thickness of a knife's back, and fill into the cases; press in and fill the cases with dry beans or peas (this is to prevent the pastry from rising and losing its shape). Bake in moderate oven. When shells are cool, they can be filled with any of the following:

1.) Spread with apricot jam and put in various drained fruit compôte or a small piece of pineapple, a cherry, half an apricot, a greengage, a plum, fresh or tinned raspberries or strawberries. Cover with thinned apricot jam.

171

2.) In place of the jam, line the pastry cases with a tablespoon of thick vanilla crême (see at the end of this recipe), put either one or several kinds of fruit on top, pipe a circle of whipped cream around it.

3.) Fill the cases with slightly sweetened whipped cream and decorate tightly with fresh strawberries or raspberries.

4.) Whisk 4 egg whites stiffly adding two tablespoons of icing sugar gradually, and one teaspoon of raspberry or redcurrant jelly. This must be really stiff, as you now add fresh raspberries, redcurrants (stripped of their stalks naturally) or fresh strawberries. Heap into the cases and decorate with more berries.

5.) Spread with apricot jam or fill with vanilla crême, top with grapes. (To 1 lb of grapes use 5 ozs [¾ cup] sugar. Bring this sugar to the boil with ½ pint of water [1 cup].) When boiling fast, put the stemless grapes in, letting them boil up once or twice, drain and put them into the cases.) Now brush the grapes with thinned apricot jam and sprinkle chopped skinned almonds on top. Put back into the oven for a few moments, until almonds are slightly yellow.

This sweet can also be made in one large cake tin or pastry case.

Vanilla crême: 1 egg
1 oz (¼ cup) cornflour   *1 pint (2 cups) milk*
1½ ozs (4 tablespoons) sugar   *1 vanilla pod*

Mix the cornflour with the egg yolk and a little of the milk. Bring the rest of the milk to the boil with one vanilla pod and the sugar, then add the cornflour and yolk mixture. Whisk continuously and cook for a few minutes. Whisk the egg white and fold into vanilla crême.

APPLES SLICES (Apfelschnitten)

Make the same pastry as before. Roll out to the thickness of a knife's back, cut into two inch squares, then make a roll about half an inch thick and with this, form a rim round each square (sticking on with white of egg). Bake in moderate oven, after having brushed over each square and rim with white of egg. Take out of oven, brush with warmed apricot jam, arrange on top 1 lb of sliced apples which you have stewed with a little water, lemon rind, lemon juice and sugar. (They should already be cool.) Top this with Meringue mixture, which you either spoon or pipe on.

Meringue:

4 egg whites are whisked stiffly, 9 ozs of icing sugar (1¼ cups) are gradually whisked in until quite stiff. Put the cake back into the oven until meringue is slightly yellowed.

RASPBERRY SLICES (Himbeerschnitten)

Is made the same way, fresh or frozen raspberries are substituted for the apples. Again top with Meringue.

REDCURRANT SLICES (Ribiselschnitten)

Currants are stripped from their stalks and used as the raspberries above. Top with Meringue.
Both raspberries and redcurrants can be put on slabs of sponge cake in the same way and then topped with the Meringue mixture.

COTTAGE CHEESE PASTRY (Topfenteig)

10 ozs (1¼ cups) butter   *10 ozs (1²/₃ cup) flour*
10 ozs cottage cheese

On a pastryboard, mix the sieved cottage cheese thoroughly with the butter and flour, add a pinch of salt. When this paste is quite smooth, form into a ball, put into a cloth and into the icebox for one hour. Then put back on pastryboard, roll out, again form into a ball, put back into the cloth and icebox for twenty minutes. Repeat this procedure four times, when it will only then be ready for use. Roll out to the thickness of a knife's back, cut into three inch squares, put a dash of jam into the middle, brush rim with egg white, fold over into a triangle, squeeze the ends together gently, brush with egg white again, and bake in medium oven.

GUGLHUPF

Used to form the most important part of a Viennese "Jause" — served at 5 o'clock, and consisting of milk coffee topped with whipped cream, and a piece of Guglhupf.

There are several ways of making Guglhupf, one is the yeast kind I have already mentioned, and then it can also be made from a sponge cake mixture and coated with chocolate icing, but the most usual kind is as follows:

5 ozs (11 tablespoons)   *5 ozs (³/₄ cup) sugar*
5 eggs   *¼ pint milk (½ cup)*
1 oz raisins   *10 ozs (slightly less than 1 cup) of*
1 tablespoon baking powder   *flour*
1 oz vanilla icing sugar   *butter and flour for the form*

Cream the butter thoroughly with one whole egg and 4 yolks. Add the sugar, the grated yellow outer peel of one lemon, the milk, half the quantity of flour and the raisins. Now whisk the 4 egg whites; when they are stiff, stir the rest of the flour mixed with the baking powder into this, and then everything into the first mixture. Pour into the buttered and floured baking tin or form, bake for one hour in moderate oven. Turn out and sprinkle with icing sugar while still hot.

MARBLE GUGLHUPF (Marmor Guglhupf)

Is made exactly like the above, except for the following: the raisins are omitted and 2 ozs of cocoa which you have mixed with a little water into a smooth paste, are mixed to half of the dough. Butter and flour a cake tin, and then alternately spoon in some of the white mixture, then some of the cocoa mixture, until all is used up.

BISHOP'S BREAD (Bischofsbrot)

5 ozs (³/₄ cup) sugar
6 eggs
3 ozs (³/₄ cup) butter
   the grated peel of 1 lemon
½ oz chopped plain chocolate

1 oz chopped candied peel
5 ozs (1¼ cup) flour
2 ozs almonds
1 oz raisins

Cream the egg yolks with the sugar, the finely grated lemon peel, the almonds (skinned and sliced thinly) the raisins, the chopped candied peel, and the small chunks of chocolate (no larger than a pea), then add the whisked egg whites, the flour and the melted butter. Put into an oblong cake tin, which you have buttered and floured. This is an excellent tea cake.

PUFF PASTRY (Blätter- oder Butterteig)

8 ozs flour
8 ozs butter
2 tablespoons white wine or
lemonjuice or mild wine vinegar

approx. ¼ cup water
a pinch of salt
1 egg yolk

On a pastryboard cut the butter into small pieces and mix this into one third of the flour. Do this with a knife and be careful not to touch the dough with your hands. Of the remaining two thirds of the flour, make a paste with the wine or vinegar and the egg yolk. Cover this with an upturned saucepan, making sure that no air can get to it. Shape into a brick and put into the icebox for an hour. Now put the secound pastry (the one without the butter) onto a board and see if it has the right soft and smooth consistency, add a little of the water if necessary. Now roll out, and into the middle of this, place the butterbrick, fold the other pastry round it so that the butterbrick is completely covered, then roll out again as one dough. Cover with a cloth and put into the icebox for half an hour. Now put on the lightly floured pastry board. Fold together again and roll out, fold together again, cover with cloth and put back into the icebox. Do this 5 to 6 times, then the pastry is ready for use. The points to watch are:

1. that you work in a cool place,
2. that no flour from the pastryboard gets folded in (it should always be brushed off),
3. that the puff pastry always goes into a hot oven,
4. that the baking sheet is not buttered, only rinsed in cold water which should not be wiped off.

Now for its uses:

CREAM SLICES (Crêmeschnitten)

Puff pastry is rolled out very thinly and cut into long strips of about 3 inches width. Bake in hot oven after having brushed the slices with egg white. Take out and cover with thick vanilla crême (see under Obsttörtchen) or with stiffly whipped cream. Top with the other strip and cut into convenient rectangular slices, dust the top sheet with icing sugar.

APPLES IN DRESSINGGOWNS (Äpfel im Schlafrock)

Approx. 2 lbs small apples   *4 ozs jam*
3 ozs (slightly less than ½ cup)   *1 egg*
sugar

Roll out the puff pastry to about a fifth of an inch thickness, cut into as many squares as you have apples. The apples (which should preferably be of a kind that do not fall too easily apart when cooked) are cored, peeled and stewed in a little water, lemon juice and sugar. When cool, fill the opening with jam and place an apple on each square, put the four ends together and pinch them gently. Brush with a beaten egg, put on a moistened baking sheet and bake in a hot oven.

JAM CRESCENTS (Marmeladekipferln)

Prepare squares as in "Äpfel im Schlafrock", put a generous dash of jam in the middle, fold together and shape like a crescent. Bake in hot oven on a moistened sheet.

PALM LEAVES (Palmenblätter)

Puff Pastry is rolled out thinly into a length double its with. Cover this thickly with coarse sugar and roll up starting from both narrow sides at the same time (as you would a Swiss roll) so that the two rolls touch in the middle. Now cut with a knife (inserting into hot water each time before cutting) into slices less than ¼ of an inch thick. Put these slices on a moistened baking sheet and bake in a hot oven until crisp and golden.

APFELSTRUDEL MADE WITH PUFF PASTRY
(Apfelstrudel aus Blätterteig)

Puff pastry is rolled out thinly and then covered with thinly sliced apples sprinkled with sugar and cinnamon, fold together (do not r o l l as other strudels!) brush with egg white and bake in hot oven. Other fillings which can be used: Poppyseeds, Cottage cheese, Nuts (see under Strudels for this); alternatively, fill with apricot slices instead of apples.

Puff pastry is also excellent for savoury use (see under Sandwiches for various fillings) it can also be served as a pastry case for a variety of fillings (see under Entrées).

WHIPPED CREAM PASTRIES (Schlagoberspastetchen)

Roll puff pastry out, cut into rounds with pastry cutter. If you use one measuring 3½ inches in diameter, cut only half of the pastry to this size. Now use a cutter slightly smaller (2½ to 3 inches in diameter) and cut half of the large rounds with this, so that you obtain circular rings. The small inside rounds can be used as covers or for something else (for example, see under cheese pastries in Sandwiches). Now put the rings on top of the rounds with a little egg white, and bake on moistened sheet in hot oven. The shells are filled with whipped cream to which you can add strawberries, or raspberries or pineapple splinters.

CHOCOLATE SALAMI (Schokoladesalami)

3 ozs plain chocolate
3 ozs almonds
1 oz candied lemon or other peel
1 oz skinned hazelnuts

½ cup rum
1 oz candied peel (orange is best if it is available)
1 egg

Grind the unskinned almonds, the hazelnuts remain whole. Chop the candied peel finely, grind the chocolate. Now put the chocolate into a doubleboiler, whisk with the egg and the rum, add all the nuts and the candied peel. Stir well on flame, but do not let it boil. Put some icing sugar on your pastryboard, put the mixture onto it and form into a "salami" coating well with icing sugar; leave to dry. Coat with chocolate icing (see under Sachertorte). Cut into thin slices for serving.

PARISIAN CREME (Pariser Crême)

½ pint (1 cup) thick cream   *½ lb good plain chocolate*

Put into a saucepan and boil up once. Then put into a double boiler and whisk continuously until a thread forms on the inserted spoon. Take the utmost care here that not even the smallest drop of water in the double boiler gets into the crême — this can be catastrophic! Now take off the burner and continue stirring until quite cold. Put into a flat dish and into the icebox. It can be eaten like this with sponge fingers — I warn you it is v e r y rich, but so good!

Can also be used for the following:

ZAUNERSTOLLEN

Make a Parisian crême as above and when stirred cool, add to this:

3 ozs wafers (the ones you   *4 ozs skinned hazelnuts (for*
*   eat with ice cream)*   *   skinning, see under Essentials)*

These amounts are used for 1½ lbs of Parisian crême. Roast the hazelnuts, and when cool, grind them finely, crush the wafers into small fragments and mix all this into the crême. If you possess a Rehrücken form (a fluted long cake tin) use this, if not, an ordinary cake tin is brushed with fine tasteless oil, and the mixture is filled in and left in the icebox for 24 hours. Take out and cover with lukewarm chocolate icing (see under Sachertorte). Put back into icebox and serve cold. Cut with a sharp knife at the table.

ZAUNERKRAPFEN

Use the same pastry as for OBSTTÖRTCHEN, only cut the rolled out pastry with a pastry cutter into small rounds (about 2 inches in diameter). Bake on a baking sheet, when cool, pipe a pointed mound of Parisian crême onto each and then put into the coldest part of your ice-box. Take out after 10 to 12 hours and ice with chocolate icing (see under Sachertorte) which should only be lukewarm. Put back into ice-box and serve when quite set.
You might find it easier to bake in one round, the size of your cake tin with a rim, and then fill in with the crême and continue as above.

CHOCOLATE SWISS ROLL (Schokolade-Roulade)

6 egg whites	2 egg yolks
3 tablespoons sugar	2½ ozs ground plain chocolate
1 tablespoon cornflour	(½ cup)
½ pint whipped cream	

Whisk the egg whites with the sugar very stiffly, then stir in carefully the egg yolks, the flour and the chocolate. On a baking sheet, place a sheet of greaseproof paper and spread the chocolate mixture on this to about ½ inch thickness. Put into hot oven and bake — this takes about 15 minutes. When ready, put on pastryboard, take the paper off and roll together. Leave to cool. Now fill with whipped cream and roll together again. You can add flavouring to the whipped cream as follows: alternatively 3 ozs grated plain chocolate or 2 tablespoons powdered coffee with or without some grated walnuts (about 2 tablespoons and 1 tablespoons of icing sugar) or 2 tablespoons strawberry jam.

WALNUT SWISS ROLL (Nußroulade)

6 eggs
2 ozs walnuts

2 ozs flour (½ cup)
½ pint whipped cream

Cream the egg yolks with the sugar, whisk the egg whites stiffly, mix carefully with the flour and the grated walnuts and mix both gently together. Put a sheet of greaseproof paper onto a baking sheet, put the mixture on it about half an inch thick, then into a hot oven for about 15 minutes. Place on a pastryboard, take off paper, roll together and leave to cool. Now roll together again with a filling of whipped cream to which you have added 3 ozs of plain grated chocolate or two teaspoons of powdered coffee. If liked, ice with coffee icing: 7 ozs icing sugar (1¾ cups) half an egg white and a little boiling water are stirred together until it has reached the right consistency, now add a few drops of strong black coffee or two teaspoons of coffee powder. Fresh strawberries mixed with whipped cream also make an excellent filling — in this case, white icing should be used.

WALNUT PASTRIES (Nußbäckerei)

5 ozs sugar (¾ cup)
6 eggs
4 ozs grated walnuts

1 oz spongecake crumbs (3 heaped tablespoons)

Cream the yolks with the sugar, then mix the ground walnuts, the spongecake crumbs and the stiffly whisked egg whites into the mixture. Cover a baking sheet with greaseproof paper and spread the mixture onto this to about half an inch thickness. Put into hot oven and bake for about 15 minutes. Take out, put on pastryboard, take off the paper and cut into rounds with a pastrycutter or into squares with a sharp knife. When cool, spread with redcurrant jam and put two and two together. For an extra finishing touch, stick on top half a walnut with some egg white. They can be filled with coffee or chocolate crème (the recipe for which you will find under "Gateaux"), and also covered with chocolate icing (see under Sachertorte in Gateaux).

GATEAUX

We have come to the part of the book which is the most Viennese of all! If you have been in Vienna you'll certainly know what I am talking about, because you will have undoubtedly paid a visit to one or two of our famous cake and pastry shops. Ah, these cake shops! We call them "Konditorei" and one could write poems about them (I think Vienna is the only place where poetry about food really is written!). Don't smile — good cooking c a n be like poetry, and even in this age of slimming one can make the best of a meal. Balanced menus with an eye on the calories are essential, but one can still organise everything so that it is arranged and served in a way which makes it a treat and a pleasant interruption to our everyday life. And what better interruption than to sit down to a delicious cake in a pastry shop! In Vienna you can look into the windows of these shops every afternoon and see them there: housewives enjoying half an hour's rest in between their shopping, business women seeking refuge there from their male working world, shopgirls having their first "sit down" of the day, and even the pangs of love can be sweetened a little — for life certainly looks less glum if you munch a slice of nutcake. Try it! Take a book, help yourself to a good piece of cake out of the icebox, relax, take a chair or better still, your chaise longue, let the cream melt in your mouth and pamper yourself a little..Forget your waistline for once — eat less bread and potatoes, cut the sugar in your tea or coffee, if you forget the calories once in a while it should always be for something worthwhile. Don't you agree? ... then "bon appetit!"

WOODCOCK CAKE (Waldschnepfentorte)

4 eggs
6 egg yolks
1/2 lb butter (1 cup)

1/2 lb sugar (1¼ cups)
1/2 lb chocolate
50 sponge fingers or 1 sponge cake.

Put the eggs, the yolks and the sugar into a double boiler, add the melted chocolate and beat over a small flame until quite thick. Take off the flame an when slightly cool, but not quite cold, stir in the butter, and then stir until the crême is quite cool. Line a cake tin with cut slices of sponge cake or sponge fingers, sprinkle with a little milk which you have mixed with a little brandy, just enough to moisten the sponge a little. Now put on the crême, another layer of sponge, moisten again, more crême and so on. Put in the icebox for a few hours but take out at least half an hour before serving, cover with whipped cream and decorate with chocolate shavings.

SPONGE FINGER CAKE (Malakofftorte)

50 sponge fingers
½ lb butter (1¼ cups)
½ lb icing sugar (1 cup)
½ cup whipped cream

½ pint milk
½ cup rum
various tinned fruit (pineapples,
strawberries, peaches)

Line a cake tin with one layer of sponge fingers which you first dip
quickly into a mixture of milk and the rum. Then put in a layer
of the crême, some of the cut fruit, another layer of sponge fingers, again dipped into the rum and milk mixture, then crême, then
fruit. The top should be crême as well as the sides, which you cover
when you have taken the cake out of the tin. The crême is made
in the following way: Mix the butter very well with the sugar, beat
until foamy, and add the whipped cream. Put the cake into the
icebox, it should be well chilled before serving.

GRILLAGE TORTE

Grillage:
6 ozs almonds
6 ozs sugar (not quite 1 cup)
Cake:
3 ozs butter (⅓ cup and
   1 tablespoon)
3 yolks

5 ozs sugar (¾ cup)
5 ozs flour (1¼ cup)
3 egg whites
1½ tablespoons baking powder
½ cup milk
1 pint whipped cream

First prepare the Grillage in the following way: skin the almonds
(see Essentials) and then chop them. In a saucepan, melt the sugar
and when it becomes yellow add the chopped almonds, when these
are also very lightly browned, put on an oiled pastry board to cool.
Put a clean cloth over the almonds and sugar mixture and pound
them with a rolling pin or a wooden meat pounder. When you have
achieved fairly small pieces put half the quantity aside and keep
for decoration. The other half put through the nut grinding machine or pound until quite fine (about the fineness of breadcrumbs).
Now in a basin mix the butter and the sugar, add the egg yolks,
lastly the fine grillage, the flour mixed with the baking powder
and the milk. At the very end add the stiffly beaten egg whites.
Butter and flour a cake tin, put the mixture in and bake slowly for
about half to three quarters of an hour. When the cake is cooled,
cut into half, fill and cover with whipped cream and decorate with
the larger grillage fragments which you have kept aside.

184

SCHÖNBRUNNERTORTE

4 eggs
3 ozs sugar (not quite ½ cup)
3 ozs plain chocolate
9 heaped tablespoons ground
  almonds

Filling:
3 ozs butter (¹/₈ cup and
  1 tablespoon)
3 ozs vanilla icing sugar (not
  quite ½ cup)
3 ozs plain chocolate
1 egg
½ cup redcurrant jelly

First of all separate the eggs, grind the chocolate, spoon it into the
eggs and sugar, continue to stir, add the ground almonds (unskinned). Cream the sugar and the egg yolks, lastly, the stiffly beaten
egg whites. Butter and flour a cake tin, put in the mixture and
bake in a medium oven for ½ to ¾ hour. Take out and cool.
Cut cake in half and spread first with redcurrant jelly, very thinly,
then with the crême. Put together, top with redcurrant jelly again
and cover top and sides with the crême, decorate by making lines
with a fork. The crême is made as follows: Melt the chocolate,
cream it with the butter and the sugar, when this is mixed well add
the egg, stir for quite some time until it becomes light and foamy.

INDIANERTORTE

6 eggs
4 ozs flour

4 ozs sugar
½ pint whipped cream

Beat the egg whites very stiffly. Stir in the yolks gradually and
carefully. Now stir in the sugar and lastly the flour. Bake in three
parts, put together with whipped cream and ice with chocolate
icing.

CHOCOLATE CAKE (Bitterschokoladetorte)

5 eggs	*Crême:*
3 ozs sugar	1 pint whipped cream
3 ozs chocolate	3 ozs chocolate

Beat the egg yolks with the sugar, add the melted chocolate and the whites of eggs which you have beaten very stiffly. Put into a buttered and floured cake tin, bake slowly in moderate oven. Fill with the following which is also used for covering: Whip the cream and mix with the melted chocolate. The cake should also be covered with this. If a slightly less rich cake is preferred, simply use plain whipped cream.

GROG GATEAU (Punschtorte)

Make a sponge cake (see recipe) enough for two round cakes. One of which you halve, and the other cut into small cubes. The cubes are put into a basin and covered with the following mixture:
Wash one orange and one lemon. Dry, and rub lumps of sugar on both their rinds, as soon as one lump is completely covered in rind put into saucepan and take the next. (You should use about 4 ozs lump sugar.) To this you add the juice of the lemon and the orange and slightly less than ½ cup of water. Bring to the boil until a thin thread forms at the end of a spoon. Now add three tablespoons of rum to this and pour over the diced sponge cubes. Mix well, add 1 tablespoon of apricot jam. Now spread the sponge cake which you have cut in half with apricot jam on both sides, put in the filling (the sponge rum mixture) and cover with the second half. Top with pink icing.

SPONGE HEDGEHOG (Biskottenigel)

25 sponge fingers	2 ozs almonds
½ lb butter (1¼ cups)	4 ozs chocolate
4 ozs sugar (½ cup)	

Melt the chocolate, stir in the butter and cream thoroughly with the sugar. On a plate, put the sponge fingers in the shape of a pointed egg. Put on a layer of crême, a layer of sponge fingers, the whole being about 4 inches high, and should have the shape of a hedgehog. Then cover with the rest of the chocolate crême, skin the almonds, cut into about 3 or 4 pieces lengthways and put into the hedgehog for spikes. You can also put in 2 glacé cherries for eyes.

STRAWBERRY CAKE (Erdbeetorte)

5 ozs butter (1/2 cup and
3 tablespoons)
5 ozs flour (1¼ cups)

10 eggs
5 ozs plain chocolate
5 ozs sugar (¾ cup)

Cream the butter thoroughly, add the sugar and the melted chocolate. Add the yolks, one after the other, whisk the egg whites stiffly, to this add the flour, now mix everything together and put into a buttered and floured cake tin. Bake in a medium oven for 1½ hours. Turn out onto a wire rack or tray and cool. Cover with whipped cream, it should be covered on the sides, but the cream should be an inch high on the top. Now cover the cream with strawberries. The small wild or garden kind are best for this, but dry large ones can also be used if they are halved or quartered. Serve at once.

I   POPPYSEED GATEAU (Mohntorte)

5 ozs butter (1/2 cup and
3 tablespoons)
5 ozs sugar (¾ cup)

2 ozs candied peel
6 eggs
5 ozs finely grated poppyseeds

Cream the butter thoroughly, add the sugar and the six egg yolks, one after the other, then add the finely cut peel, the poppyseeds and the stiffly beaten egg whites. Put into buttered and floured cake tin and bake for one hour. Sprinkle liberally with icing sugar while still hot.

II   MOHNTORTE

Is made the same way, 2 ounces of plain melted chocolate are added to the mixture, and the peel is substituted by two ounces of grated unskinned almonds. When cool, this cake is covered thinly with apricot jam and chocolate icing (see under Sachertorte).

CLUBGATEAU (Clubtorte)

½ lb butter (1¼ cups)   5 eggs
½ lb icing sugar (1 cup)   1 large sponge cake

This cake you can either prepare with a bought sponge cake or sponge fingers, or with a sponge cake which you have made yourself with either your own favourite cake mix or a recipe from this book. Mix the butter very well with the five egg yolks and gradually stir in the sugar and lastly, the stiffly beaten egg whites. Into a large cake form fill about one inch of this crème and cover with thin slices of the sponge cake or sponge fingers, then another one inch layer of the crème, sponge cake again, and so on until you have used up both the cake and the crème. The last layer should be of crème. Put the cake into the icebox and leave there overnight. Before serving, take the cake out of the tin, put on a flat plate and cover with a pint of stiff whipped cream. Garnish the top with tiny pineapple cubes, fresh strawberries or raspberries.

The Clubtorte can be varied in the following ways:

1. Substitute Sachertorte for the sponge (or one of your Chocolate cake mixes) and Chocolate crème — the one you will find for the recipe under Schönbrunnertorte is particularly good with it.

2. Sponge cake and coffeecrème (the one given in Kaffeecrêmetorte).

3. Caramelcrème and sponge or nutcake.

SACHERTORTE

This is the most famous gateau of Vienna, which in a way is rather strange, because it differs so much from any of the other typical Viennese cakes, which are mostly very rich and creamy. You may have heard one of the many stories concerning the Sachertorte, and how and why it was first created. There are quite a number in existence, and of course everyone claims that his or her story is the only true version. To this I must add mine, which goes like this: The famous Prince Metternich, who was one of the leading statesmen of the Vienna Congress, once said to Mr. Sacher, who was the founder of the well-know hotel. "— Why don't you make a plainer and more masculine gateau? All these rich creamy crea-

tions are only for sweet-toothed women." So Mr. Sacher made up the recipe for the following cake, and a very successful creation it proved to be:

5 ozs butter (½ cup and
   3 tablespoons)
5 ozs sugar (¾ cup)
5 ozs chocolate
8 egg yolks
10 egg whites

4 ozs flour (1 cup)
2 ozs apricot jam

Covering:
6 ozs sugar (1 cup)
6 ozs finest plain chocolate

Beat the butter until quite fluffy, melt the chocolate in the oven, add this together with the sugar to the creamed butter. Add the egg yolks one after the other. Whisk the egg whites stiffly, fold in the flour and mix this carefully with the first mixture. Butter a cake tin, flour lightly, fill in with the mixture and bake slowly in a medium oven for 1½ hours. When baked, take out, put on a wire tray and theen turn at once onto another one, it is essential that this cake cools in the same position in which it was baked. When cool, cut top flat so that it can stand on this side, as the bottom part is used for covering, and must be quite smooth. Warm the apricot jam slightly, spread over the cake and cover with the chocolate icing.

Chocolate icing: Bring the sugar to the boil with slightly less than ½ cup of water, cook until it forms a thin thread at the end of an inserted wooden spoon, add the melted chocolate, mix well, there must be no lumps. Keep stirring until mixture is thick enough to pour over the cake. Leave to set and serve whipped cream in a bowl separately with the cake.

189

COFFEE CREME GATEAU (Kaffeecrêmetorte)

5 ozs sugar	*Crème:*
5½ ozs almonds	4 yolks
4 egg whites	3 ozs icing sugar
3 ozs butter	3 tablespoons strong coffee
	3 ozs butter

Beat the egg whites stiffly. The almonds should be blanched and cut finely.Add to the egg whites and gradually add the sugar. Bake in 3 parts and the last sprinkle with cut almonds and sugar. When cool, fill with the following crème. In a double boiler beat the four egg yolks, the sugar and the coffee until thick. When cool, add the creamed butter. Fill into the cake, the top layer should of course be the one with the cut almonds.

CHEESECAKE (Topfentorte)

5 ozs butter (½ cup and	5 ozs sugar (¾ cup)
3 tablespoons)	4 ozs blanched grated almonds
6 eggs	2 tablespoons breadcrumbs
7 ozs cream or cottage cheese	

Cream the butter, add the sugar, the egg yolks, the juice of half a lemon and the finely grated peel of one lemon (the yellow part only). Whisk the egg whites, to this add the grated almonds and add to the first mixture, to which you have stirred the cream cheese. Mix gently with the egg whites. Put into a buttered and floured cake tin and bake in medium oven very slowly.

CHESTNUTS

I don't think anywhere (with the possible exception of Spain or Italy where they are grown) are such delightful dishes concocted from chestnuts as here in Austria. Incidentally, Chestnut vendors are the only type of the old Street vendors depicted in the "Cries of Vienna" who still exist. It gives a special glow to a dull November day to see those little charcoal ovens, and the men or women tending them muffled up to the ears and in enormous boots; one feels that things are still alright, they are here again, and at least one thing remains the same! And as one goes down the street munching happily, it always is a particular foretaste of Christmas.

The best way to shell the chestnuts is as follows: Make a slit across the middle, be careful only to cut the skin, as they easily break once the nut itself is cut. Heat oven "medium" and put chestnuts on a baking sheet for a few minutes, then take them out and take their outer shell off together with the brown skin. This must be done while they are still hot, as the brown skin sticks when they are cool.

KASTANIENREIS

2 lbs chestnuts   *½ lb sugar (½ cup)*
1 pint milk (2 cups)

Put the shelled chestnuts into the milk and simmer until they are soft. Now drain and take one eighth of a pint of the milk and spin with the sugar (a small thread must form). Put the chestnuts through a sieve, add the sugar, mix and beat will with a wooden spoon. When the mixture is cool put into a potatoricer or meatmincer and force through into a glass bowl or individual sundae glasses. Top with whipped cream (about half a pint) and some glacé cherries.

MOCK CHESTNUTS (Falsche Kastanien)

Half the quantity as in last recipe and treat the same way until the point where one mixes with the sugar. Now take a little of the mixture (about the size of a walnut) and form a chestnut out of it. Insert a toothpick, or better still, a cocktailstick at the end, and dip into melted covering chocolate, so that only the end part remains uncovered, to resemble the light part of the real chestnut. To dry, stick the chestnuts into a loaf of bread, then remove the sticks and put into candy papers.

CHESTNUT BREAD (Kastanienbrot)

½ lb sugar (¼ cup)   Cocoa
2 lbs chestnuts   1 pint milk (2 cups)

Treat the chestnuts as in the first recipe and divide the mixture into two halves. Into the first half add as much cocoa until the mixture becomes quite dark, add a little cream if it is too hard to form. Now shape into a long sausage on an equally long narrow plate. Out of the remaining mixture, to which you have also added a little cream, you form a sheet with which you cover the dark part. This looks very attractive when cut.

CHESTNUT BRICK (Kastanienziegel)

1 lb chestnuts   ½ lb sugar = ½ cup
1 cup milk   (¼ lb for the chestnuts,
½ lb almonds   ¼ lb for the almonds)

Treat Chestnuts in the usual way. Form low brick which you spread with raspberry or redcurrant jam.
This you cover with almond paste. The almonds are peeled, dried in a warm oven, grated finely and mixed with the sugar, a teaspoon of white of egg and a drop of maraschino. Knead well and cover chestnut brick. If desired, the almond paste can be dyed pink or green with a little coloring.

SPONGECAKE (Biscuit)

5 ozs butter (½ cup and
  3 tablespoons)
5 ozs cornflour (1¼ cups)

6 eggs
5 ozs sugar (¾ cup)

Cream the butter and add the egg yolks. Whisk the egg whites stiffly, stir in the sugar carefully. Alternating with the cornflour which is added to the eggs and the butter. Do everything gently and lightly. Butter and flour a cake tin, pour in the mixture, bake in a medium oven.

This can be the base for all recipes which require spongecakes or spongefingers, it can also be cut and filled with any of the crêmes mentioned with other cakes.

I have purposely not given you oven temperatures or baking times, I have taken it for granted that you already cook to an average standard, and as all ovens vary, it is better that I leave this to your own discretion — you are bound to know your own oven and its moods better than I!

FRUIT GATEAU (Obsttorte)

6 ozs butter (⁵/₆ cup)
6 eggs
6 ozs sugar (⁴/₅ cup)
6 ozs flour (1½ cups)

Icing:
Juice of ½ lemon
½ cup water
8 ozs icing sugar (1¼ cups)
7 ozs granulated or lump sugar

Cream the butter, add the six eggs, cream a little longer and then add the sugar, lastly the flour. Butter a cake tin and fill in with the mixture — bake slowly for about 40 minutes. Take out and place on a wire rack or tray, and when cool spread with orange marmalade, about a finger's breadth high. Now take any compôte or canned fruit (if you take canned, don't take the mixed kind, but open a can of each). Starting with the outer edge, make a circle of peach halves, then a circle of cherries, then apricots and so on. The fruit should be well drained. Secure the fruit with toothpicks before you cover with the icing. When you have secured the first circle of peaches, it is then easier to arrange the rest of the fruit, pineapples, greengages, cherries, apricots or any other firm fruit. Do all this while the cake is still on the wire tray.

Icing.

Melt the lump sugar with the water in a saucepan, bring to the boil and cook until a thread forms on an inserted wooden spoon, take away from heat. In a basin mix the icing sugar with the juice of the lemon and into this stir the first sugar mixture which is now lukewarm. Continue stirring until it has the right consistency for icing. Now spoon the icing liberally over the cake and the fruit. At first it will run off, so you will have to repeat the process several times. The icing also has to be continually warmed so that it remains liquid. When everything is well covered, leave to dry, then remove the toothpicks.

Cocktail Titbits and Sandwiches

FOR COCKTAILS AND OPEN SANDWICHES

Now I can really anticipate your reaction — for Cocktails certainly can't be labelled Austrian, however, I won't talk about drinks, but I do have a few tips for various tasty cocktail "accessories". The hot ones can also be made on a slightly larger scale and served as the main course with vegetables. The base is in most cases a Crouton, which is a round slice of buttered toast.

1.) 1 crouton, 1 porksteak, a thin slice of boiled ham, a swirl or Sauerkraut into which you put a small fried potato.

2.) 1 buttered crouton, 1 tiny beefsteak, 1 fried mushroom. Pipe a circle of creamed potatoes around the mushroom, top with horseradish sauce.

3.) 1 buttered crouton, 1 small beefsteak, 1 slice of ham, 1 small sprig of cooked cauliflower. Put a small drop of tomato ketchup on the cauliflower, pipe a circle of mayonnaise around it.

4.) 1 buttered crouton, 1 vealsteak, the "fond" of 1 artichoke which you fill with chopped hardboiled egg and a spoonful of mayonnaise.

5.) 1 buttered crouton, 1 piece of fried liver, 1 slice of boiled ham, 1 slice of fried tomato, top with fried onion rings.

6.) 1 slice of Semmelknödel (bread-dumpling) fried on both sides, 1 small vealsteak, ½ fried tomato, the small heart of a lettuce dipped in dressing.

7.) 1 small pastry case filled with cranberry jelly, 1 small venison-steak, top with 1 slice of orange.

8.) 1 pastry case filled with sliced fried veal kidneys, 1 small veal-steak topped with green beans with a little melted butter dripped on them.

9.) 1 boiled onion (it should be large enough to hold a small venisonsteak) is flattened at the bottom so that it will stand up. Now put the venionsteak on it and spread this with a little tomato ketchup, then a few sautéed sliced mushrooms and top with an olive.

10.) Hirnpofesen (Brains on toast, see under Offal).

All the ingredients must be hot, the steaks should be fried quickly on both sides, the croutons must be fried freshly in the butter and then are topped in the given order. They are best served hot on a platter which can be put on a heater on the buffet table.

SANDWICHES

Viennese Sandwiches are nearly always the "open" kind, and because of this, allow for considerably more variety. The variations already begin with the bread, and the number of possibilities with which you can vary the bases for these sandwiches is enormous! The most important detail of the open sandwich, is that the butter reaches the edge of the bread, and that whatever is put on top covers this completely.

For "mixed" open sandwiches, any kind of bread is used. The bread is buttered, then slices of ham, any kind of sausage, cheese, sliced hardboiled egg, gherkins are added. The size of the slice is to your own individual taste, also the decoration, it can be piped with mayonnaise or diced aspic jelly can also be used. The bread is cut into halves, squares, triangles or with your own pastry cutter. If you are slicing from a small loaf, you won't need to cut them at all, but I would advise you to remove the crust. This type of sandwich is served in every simple Viennese home, the exact form of presentation depends of course on the individual house-wife — everyone has a different "touch" where these things are concerned.

T i m e s at which they are served vary considerably, they can appear at "tea-time", or as a simple cold supper with a glass of

wine, or even if you are invited a f t e r the evening meal. In a more sophisticated home, one will find the more unusual type of sandwich combinations. Let me give you a few ideas for these:

First a simple "closed sandwich" which you might not be familiar with:

> Between two thinly sliced buttered slices of white bread put a thin slice of darkest rye. It sounds and is, simple, but tastes delicious!

Now for some open sandwiches:

1.) Spread brown bread with butter to which you have added either crushed anchovies or anchovy paste, cut into narrow slices, add a row of hardboiled eggs (sliced), decorate with piped tomato purée and capers.

2.) Onto a semi-sweet white bread, buttered, scrape a little french mustard, cover with thin ham slices, decorate with chopped gherkins and aspic cubes.

3.) Mix the butter with freshly grated horseradish, cover semi-sweet white bread freely with this, then with smoked tongue; pipe with mayonnaise coloured green with minced spinach.

4.) Cover white bread with a green mayonnaise (see above) make roses of smoked salmon slices (cut into half inch strips and roll up) set on the green mayonnaise.

5.) Cover white bread with pink mayonnaise (add tomato purée or ketchup to mayonnaise) put canned asparagus tips on top, in one direction, then a thin strip of smoked salmon or tomato across the asparagus to give the impression of a tied ribbon.

6.) Mix roquefort cheese with butter, put on white or rye bread, to half an inch thickness, decorate by drawing a thin fork across and with walnut halves.

7.) On a slice of toast covered with a thick mayonnaise, arrange a cluster of cooked vegetables (green peas, carrot slices a sprig of cauliflower, a few asparagus tips). Pipe with thick mayonnaise.

8.) On white or dark bread spread thickly with Liptauer cheese (see under Cold Entrées) arrange radish slices overlapping one another, decorate with parsley.

9.) Butter dark rye bread, cover with scrambled eggs (cool) decorate with small tomato slices and chopped paprika, peppers.

10.) On lightly buttered dark rye bread spread a thick mixture of cream cheese, to which you have added finely chopped green paprika, salt, pepper and a pinch of paprika powder, decorate with tomato strips.

11.) A piece of white toast is spread with a thick mayonnaise to which you have added some cooked tiny peas, cover with slices of chicken meat — a little of the mayonnaise should remain visible.

12.) Butter is mixed with french mustard, dark rye bread is covered with this and rolls of thinly cut roast beef are arranged over this. A slice of pickled cucumber is inserted in each beef roll, pipe a line of green mayonnaise between each.

13.) Mix very finely chopped aspic with mayonnaise spread on white toast, arrange shrimps on this, decorate with fresh cucumber slices, which you halve and stand on edge between the shrimps.

14.) Butter a slice of dark rye bread thinly, mix more butter thoroughly with sardines and cover the bread generously with this; decorate with gherkin slices.

15.) Cream cheese is mixed with mayonnaise and chopped dill. Spread a slice of white bread thickly with this, cover with small pieces of boiled fresh or canned salmon and fresh cucumber strips.

16.) To a thick mayonnaise, add some drained and minced beetroot, cover a slice of white bread with this, then with strips of cold venison or roastbeef.

17.) To a thick mayonnaise, add hardboiled chopped eggs (to a thick enough consistency for spreading on a piece of white bread), decorate with anchovy rings.

18.) Butter a slice of white bread or toast, spread with a Sauce Cumberland or Orange (see under Sauces) cover with thinly cut slices of venison, decorate with sliced olives.

19.) Butter is mixed with diced ham, diced chopped gherkins and a little mustard. This is spread thickly on rye bread, decorate with cubes of aspic.

20.) Cream cheese or cottage cheese is mixed with butter, chopped radishes, chopped chives, chopped parsley. Spread thickly on the darkest rye bread available, decorate with sprigs of parsley.
Arrange on large Boards or platters as a colourful "mixed bag", or keeping each different kind to its own row. If you have made them all of the same size, arrange as a "chequer board". An optional finishing touch is to brush them with liquid aspic jelly (see under Essentials), it certainly gives them a professional look!

FILLED SANDWICH LOAVES

Filled loaves which are then cut into sandwiches are also a speciality of the Austrian kitchen.

Take a long white loaf and after you have cut one or both ends off and taken all the inner part out fill with any of the following stuffings:

1.) Cream butter well (it should be quite soft) and into this mix the following diced ingredients: Ham, swiss cheese, hardboiled eggs, gherkins and any cold meat you may fancy. If it is possible to include a few pistachio nuts, it makes it look even more attractive.

2.) Mix the butter with anchovy, either crushed or paste, and to this add chopped mixed pickles, pickled herrings and smoked salmon both cut into strips. Use equal parts of all ingredients.

3.) To a thick mayonnaise add an equal quantity of liquid aspic (see under Essentials) to this add skinned diced tomatoes, double their quantity of diced chicken meat and/or roast veal, a few peeled, diced gherkins (approximately the same quantity as tomatoes).

4.) Calves' liver is fried quickly with some onions and put through the mincer. To half a pound of this allow three hardboiled eggs, which are also put through the mincer. Salt and pepper are added and as much creamed butter to give the consistency of a paté. Now add a few sliced stuffed olives.

5.) To a thick mayonnaise, add an equal amount of aspic jelly, enough tomato purée to colour it pink, and to this add chopped capers, chopped gherkins, a pinch of curry and a generous quantity of cubed beef, either boiled or roast.

6.) Cream the butter with an equal quantity of sardines, add some french mustard, chopped gherkins and chopped hardboiled eggs.

These loaves are put in the ice-box for a few hours before serving, and then sliced.

SANDWICH GATEAU (Sandwichtorte)

I don't know if it is possible for you to get bread baked in a round cake shape. If you can, do so and cut the crust off all over. If its not possible to get this shape, use thin slices of white bread (at least a day old), which you put in layers into a cake tin, either round or square, or make a brick.

Divide the butter into three equal parts, cream it well for spreading; to one part add anchovy paste, to the second chopped parsley and to the third, cream cheese.

On the bottom layer spread anchovy butter, and on this put slices of hardboiled eggs, spread the next slice of bread with anchovy butter again and put on top of the eggs. Now butter the top of this with parsley butter and over this put sliced ham on which is spread a little mustard. Top with a parsley buttered slice. Over this spread cream cheese butter, and on this put a layer of smoked tongue or roastbeef on which you sprinkle grated horseradish, top with a cream cheese slice again. On the next top repeat with a spread of anchovy butter, putting on slices of smoked salmon; and so on until you have used up all slices.

Other variations with the same spreads are: sardines crushed with a little lemon juice and mustard on the anchovy butter; salami or sausage on the parsley butter; cheese on the cream cheese spread. As you can see, there is no end to the variations, but in this respect take care that it does not become too rich — guard against spreading too thickly and make sure that everything used is lean. When the "cake" is finished, put a board on top to press it down. Leave for about three hours, then remove board and "ice" the cake with cream cheese all round. The top is garnished with walnuts, salted almonds, radishroses, parsley, caviar, hardboiled eggs etc., etc.

You will have noticed that I have ,ot given you quantities for any of the Sandwiches, loaves or Sandwich cake. It depends largely on the size of loaves and appetites!

Sandwiches which are served hot.

STUFFED ROLLS

Cut off the tops of small bridge rolls (long or round) and keep aside, until filled. Take out the white part of the rolls, brush the inside with melted butter and fill with: scrambled eggs, ham filling, any of the fillings given for profiteroles or ham crescents (see Hot Entrées). Brush with beaten egg and put into a medium warm oven. Serve warm on a napkin.

All the fillings given for Ham Crescents (Schinkenkipferln — see Entrées) can also be put onto buttered toast and served as hot sandwiches.

BLÄTTERTEIG

Prepare a puff pastry (see under Cakes) and cut into rounds, squares or strips; these are brushed with beaten egg and sprinkled with either of the following: poppyseeds, carraway seeds, grated cheese and paprika.

HAMCAKE (Schinkenkuchen)

3 ozs butter (¹/₃ cup and
* 1 tablespoon)*
1 oz grated cheese

3 eggs
5 ozs chopped lean ham
* (approx. 1½ cups)*

Cream the butter with the egg yolks, the grated cheese, add the chopped ham and lastly the stiffly beaten egg whites. Butter a baking tin, fill in the mixture and bake in a medium hot oven rather slowly. Serve hot cut into slices; if liked grated cheese can be served with this.

A FEW TASTY METHODS FOR USING UP LEFTOVERS

RICE: If there is only a little, and even if it contains vegetables, it can be put into clear soup (see under Beefbroth).
If there is a larger quantity, it can be used in stuffed green peppers (see under Faschiertes) or in stuffed tomatoes.

PANCAKES: These can be used as "Fridatten" in clear soup (see under Beefbroth) or if more are left, they can be made into any of the baked pancake recipes (see under Warm Desserts).

NOODLES, MACCARONI ETC.: Can be used in clear, tomato or cheese soup (see under Soups).

DUMPLINGS: Can be cut up and put into soup (see under Soups) or can be cut up and fried with eggs (see under Plain Dishes) or can be used as a base for one of the Cocktail Titbits.

POTATOES: Tiroler Gröstl (see under Plain Dishes) or sour cream potatoes (also under Plain Dishes).

NOCKERLN: Can be used for Nockerln fried with eggs or Holz-hackernockerln (both under Plain Dishes) but they can also be warmed up in any thick sauce.

HAM: Can be made into ham pudding, baked or steamed, or can be used as a stuffing either hot or cold for tomatoes.

BOILED BEEF: Can be used cold for Gezupftes Rindfleisch (Plucked beef) or Rindfleischsalat (beef salad) — for both see under Cold Entrées; or use it cut up and fried with onions for Tiroler Gröstl or filled potato dumplings (see under Plain Dishes).

CHICKEN: See under Hühnerreis (Chicken rice) in main section of Poultry and Game. Or under "Cold Entrées": Chicken in Aspic.

VEGETABLES: Can be used as a filling for pancakes or steamed puddings. Peas, green beans, carrots if only cooked in water can be made into salads (see under Salads).

STALE WHITE BREAD OR ROLLS: Make into dumplings (see Beilagen), pofesen, or grate into breadcrumbs.

COLD VEAL, LEAN PORK OR BEEF: Make into meat salads (see Cold Entrées).

GULYAS: Can be made into Gulyas soup. Simply warm the gulyas carefully to prevent it from becoming brown, add as much beefbroth or stock as you think it will take and yet still have the right consistency. Add cubed potatoes and some chopped up Frankfurters. Alternatively, it can be used for Gulyaspancakes (see under Plain Dishes) or Gulyasstrudel (see under "Warm Entrées").

TYPICAL
AUSTRIAN MENUS

So far, I have just given you recipes with only a few suggestion's of what they should be served with. Now I shall plan a few Menus for you and divide them into three groups, the first, for Everyday, the second, with an accent on Simplicity, and the third, for Festive use.

Everyday.

1. Paradeissuppe mit Reis (Tomato soup with rice) — Gefülltes Kraut, Salzerdäpfeln (Stuffed cabbagerolls, boiled potatoes) — Schneenockerln (Whisked Nockerl and Vanilla sauce).

2. Rindsuppe mit Grießnockerln (Beef broth with Semolinanockerl) — Rindfleisch mit Oberskren, Spinat, Erdäpfelschmarren (Boiled beef with horseradish cream, creamed spinach, fried boiled potatoes) — Apfelkompott (Stewed apples).

3. Karfiolsuppe (Cauliflower soup) — Geröstete Leber mit Nudeln, grüner Salat (Fried Liver with onions, noodles, green salad) — Apfelstrudel (Apple strudel).

4. Haussulz mit Essig und Zwiebel (Pork brawn with chopped onions and dressing) — Gulyaspalatschinken (Gulyas pancakes) — Pofesen mit Zwetschkenkompott (Fritters with stewed plums).

5. Gebackenes Hirn mit Paradeissalat, Gurkensalt, Petersilerdäpfeln (Brains fried in egg and breadcrumbs, tomato salad, cucumber salad, parsley potatoes) — Weinkoch mit Chaudeau (Wine pudding with wine sauce).

6. Jägerbraten, Erdäpfeln, Erbsen- und Karottengemüse, grüner Salat (Ground mixed "Hunter's" Meatloaf, (peas and Carrots, potatoes, green salad) — Nußstrudel (Walnut yeast strudel).

7. Schwammerlsuppe (Mushroom soup) — Naturschnitzel, Fisolen, Reis, Zeller- und Erdäpfelsalat (Escallopes naturel, either pork or veal, green beans, rice, celery and potato salad mixed) — Kastanienreis mit Schlagobers (Chestnut rice with whipped cream).

8. Szegediner Krautfleisch, Salzerdäpfeln (Stewed pork à la Szegedin with white cabbage and boiled potatoes) — Apfel im Schlafrock ("Apple in a dressing-gown": apples in pastry).

9. Paprikafisch, warm mit Erdaepfeln (Hot paprikafish and potatoes) — Haselnusspudding mit Schokoladesauce (Steamed hazelnut pudding with chocolate sauce).

10. Rindsuppe mit Fridatten (Beef broth with cut pancakes) — Eingemachtes Kalbfleisch mit Bröseknödel (Veal ragout with mixed vegetables, breadcrumb dumplings) — Gleichgewichtskuchen mit Obst (Equal weight cake with fruits in season).

Now for the Simpler ones — for example, when you're lunching alone with the Children!

1. Tirolerknödel mit grünem und Paradeissalat (Tyrolean dumplings, with tomato and lettuce salad) — "Klosterschwestern" ("Nuns" — Pears and chocolate sauce).

2. Erbsensuppe mit Nockerl (Green pea soup with small Nockerl) — Schwammerl mit Ei, grüner Salat (Mushrooms and scrambled eggs with green salad) — Gebackene Mäuse mit Himbeersaft ("Fried Mice" — Yeast fritters and fruit syrup).

3. Gebackene Schinkenfleckerln, Fisolensalat (Baked ham noodles, green bean salad) — Blätterteigmohnstrudel mit Zwetschken drin (Puff pastry with plums and poppyseed filling).

4. Bouillon mit Ei (Beef broth with egg) — Topfenpalatschinkenauflauf (Baked cheese pancakes).

5. Rindfleischsalat, Paradeissalat mit grünem Paprika (Boiled beef salad, tomato salad with Green Peppers) — Reisauflauf (Baked rice pudding).

6. Käsesuppe mit Makkaroni (Cheese soup with Maccaroni) — Topfenknödel mit Zwetschkenkompott (Cream cheese dumplings with stewed plums).

7. Gulyassuppe (Gulyas soup) — Kaiserschmarren (Baked pancake batter — "Emperor's trifle").

8. Eiersalat mit Erdäpfelsalat (Egg salad with potato salad) — Marillenknödel (Apricot dumplings).

9. Letscho mit Ei (Stewed tomatoes, onions and peppers with eggs) — Germknödel mit Powidl und Mohn (Yeast dumplings with prune stuffing, ground poppyseeds and butter).

10. Erdäpfelsuppe (Potato soup) — Grießschmarren mit Kirschen (Semolina "trifle" with cherries).

Festive.

1. Rindsuppe mit Leberknödeln (Beef soup with liver dumplings) — Wiener Schnitzel mit Reis und grünen Erbserln, Mayonnaisesalat (Vienna Schnitzel with rice, green peas and Mayonnaise salad) — Waldschnepfentorte (Chocolate cream cake "Woodcock").

2. Eier in Paradeis-Mayonnaise (Eggs in Sauce Mayonnaise) — Gespickter Rehrücken mit Croquetten, Cumberland sauce (Saddle of Venison, Potato croquettes, Cumberland sauce) — Bitterschokoladetorte (Plain chocolate cake with whipped cream).

3. Karpfen in Aspik (Carp in Aspic) — Harlekinbraten mit Reis, Spargelgemüse, gemischter Salat (Roast Veal or Pork à l'Harlequin, creamed asparagus tips, mixed salad) — Sachertorte mit Schlag (Sacher cake with whipped cream).

207

4. Warmer Schinkenpudding (Hot steamed ham pudding) — Gefüllte Kalbsbrust, Paradeissalat, Reis mit Schwammerln (Stuffed breast of veal, rice with mushrooms, tomato salad) — Scheidlcrêmetorte (Buttercream cake).

5. Kalte gefüllte Paradeiser (Stuffed cold tomatoes) — Eingemachtes Huhn mit Spargeln, Erbserln und Schwämmen, kleine Semmelknödel (Creamed chicken with asparagus tips, small peas and mushrooms, small bread dumplings) — Brandteigkrapfen mit Erdbeerfülle (Profiteroles with pink icing and strawberry filling).

6. Gefüllte Eier mit Mayonnaise (Stuffed eggs and Mayonnaise) — Beefsteaks in Blätterteig, gemischter Salat (Beefsteaks in puff pastry, mixed salad) — Rehrücken mit Schlagobers (Special Chocolate cake — see under Gateaux — with whipped cream).

7. Schinkenrollen mit Oberskren (Ham rolls with grated horseradish cream filling) — Paprikahuhn mit Nockerln (Paprika boiling chicken with Nockerln) — Malakofftorte (Malakofftorte).

8. Gemüseplatte, warm (Mixed plate of vegetables with melted butter) — Schweinsbraten mit Rotkraut und Erdäpfelknödeln (Roast Pork with red cabbage, potato dumplings) — Kastanienbaumstamm (Chestnuttree).

9. Spargel, Karfiol und grüne Erbserln mit Mayonnaise (Asparagus, cauliflower, green peas with mayonnaise) — Kalbsvögerln mit Rahmsauce, Makkaroni (Rolled escallopes of Veal with cream sauce, maccaroni) — Salzburger Nockerln (Salzburger Nockerl).

10. Spargelsuppe (Asparagus soup) — Faschierter Braten mit Würstel und Eierspeis, roter Rüben- und Zellersalat, Erdäpfelpüree mit gerösteten Zwieberln, Spinat (Roast ground mixed Meat loaf filled with scrambled eggs and frankfurters, beetroot and celery salad, creamed potatoes with fried onion ringsspinach) — Kaffeecrêmetorte (Coffee crême gateau).

A Guide to Austrian Wines

HISTORY

Zagersdorf, in the region of Burgenland, is thought to be the oldest winemaking village in Austria. Wine seeds have been discovered there in an ancient grave dating back to approximately 700 B.C. It is believed that the Celts, who settled in that area around the same period and in Südsteiermark in Styria a few hundred years later, were also producing wines.

During Roman times, vine cultivation was widespread in Noricum, a Roman province in the eastern Alps (between Rhaetia, Pannonia and Italy). Goblets, pitchers and bottles have been excavated from this area and are on display in Austrian museums today. When the Romans left this area by the end of the fifth century, winemaking almost disappeared, though there is some record of it under the rule of Charlemagne (742-814).

Later a completely new wine culture developed in Austria, as Bavarian monks planted vines along the Danube River in lower Austria. Before that, vines were found mainly west of Linz, but soon they were growing on thousands of hectares to the east. One wine produced in the east was Trockenbeerenauslese, which was harvested as early as 1526 according to an old inscription on a barrel. It is also documented that the last drops of this wine were drunk in 1852.

An increase in beer consumption, along with the devastating effects of the Thirty Years War and high taxes led to a decline in wine production. Eventually, when the Empress Maria Theresa (1717-1780) standardized taxation, winemaking came to the forefront again. In 1784, Maria Theresa's son Emperor Josef II issued a decree allowing winemakers to sell wines on their own premises. Thus Austria's famous "Heurige" taverns were born. These popular "wine inns" feature wine produced on the property, usually served straight from the vat, in large flasks or jugs.

The nineteenth century saw another setback in Austrian wine production, as vineyards were destroyed by a severe freeze and plant diseases that made their way to Europe from North America. Towards the end of that century, however, wine schools were founded in the various centers of Austrian winemaking. These schools helped develop methods to combat diseases, improve quality, and establish the winemakers' reputations.

At the end of World War II, new techniques and modern equipment were introduced to Austrian vineyards, and improvements in wine production resulted. In 1985, however, a very public scandal rocked the Austrian wine industry. Some producers were found adulterating wines with diethylene glycol in order to adjust the viscosity and sweetness. They then attempted to pass these bottles off as expensive late-harvest wines. No one was injured from drinking these wines, but the credibility of Austrian wine makers was certainly tarnished in the world market. Ironically, this unpleasant incident helped lead to today's healthy and growing Austrian wine industry. The Austrian government reacted to the scandal by instituting some of the world's strictest winemaking regulations, which have inspired Austrian wine producers to make top-quality wines.

AUSTRIAN WINEMAKING TODAY

Austria produces about 2.5 million hectoliters of wine per year, making it the world's seventeenth largest wine-producing country. Both indigenous and "classic" grape varieties are grown, of which approximately 80% are white and 20% are red.

White Wines

The most famous Austrian wine is clearly Grüner Veltliner, a tart, fruity and peppery white that pairs well with seafood, white-meat dishes, and a wide range of foods. It is the most popular grape variety cultivated, accounting for over 36% of total plantings. Other white wine varieties include Riesling, Müller-Thurgau, and Weissburgunder (Pinot Blanc), with Chardonnay (known as Morillon) and even Sauvignon Blanc gaining in popularity.

Red Wines

Blauer Zweigelt, a hybrid of St. Laurent and Blaufränkisch grapes, is the most widely planted red variety, accounting for 6% of total plantings. Other reds include Blauer Portugieser, Blaufränkisch, St. Laurent (velvety and fruity), Blauburgunder (Pinot Noir), and even some Cabernet Sauvignon.

Dessert Wines

Austria's dessert wines are among the finest in the world. The most famous are the exotic ones from around Lake Neusiedl in the Burgenland region, where conditions are perfect for growing sweet, botrytis-affected grapes. *Botrytis Cinerea*, or "noble rot" as it is often called, attacks the grapes in the marshy, humid lake region every year. Thus producers can offer the famed Neusiedlersee dessert wine to connoisseurs on a regular basis. Other dessert wines include Beerenauslese, Trockenbeerenauslese, Eiswein, and Ausbruch, an indigenous type of sweet wine that is one of the world's most exotic ones.

Wine Regions

Today the wine-growing areas of Austria are all in the eastern part of the country, around the capital Vienna, covering a total area of about 60,000 hectares. There are four main regions, which each contain sub-regions.

I. Lower Austria (Niederösterreich)

This is the largest wine-growing region, covering about 34,000 hectares or 58% of the total.

Carnuntum (891 hectares) is one of the most famous sub-regions in this area. It bears the name of a Roman fortress on the border of the Danube River and Pannonia. Its ruins can be visited today just outside Bad Deutsch-Altenburg, where the archeological park and Museum Carnuntum feature Roman mosaics, pottery, and agricultural tools.
Sand, loam, gravel and loess are the main soils in this region, where whites like Grüner Veltliner, Welschriesling, Weissburgunder and Chardonnay are the primary products, but Zweigelt and St. Laurent are reds that are gaining in popularity. Carnuntum's two wine growing centers are Prellenkirchen and Göttlesbrunn.

Donauland (2731 hectares) is a major wine-growing area where vines are cultivated primarily on loess soil. Grüner Veltliner is the main product, but Rieslings and Weissburgunders (Pinot Blancs) are also popular. This area boasts a stunning and famous abbey in the historical town of Klosterneuburg. The abbey's cornerstone was laid in 1114 and its cellar was built to house superb wines from the region.

Kamptal (3868 hectares) is home to Austria's largest wine town, Langenlois. A wine-related feature of this region is the Zöbinger Heiligenstein or "Hellenstein" as it is referred to in the Zwettl Abbey register of 1280—a mountain on which the sun "burns like hell" but where the grapes are heavenly. Abundant clay, loess and primary rock soils help create the region's distinctive, peppery Grüner Veltliner.

Kremstal (2175 hectares) is home to the medieval town of Krems, which also features impressive late Gothic, Renaissance and Baroque buildings. The school for viticulture in Krems was founded in 1875 and it continues to provide education for wine students, enthusiasts and future wine professionals.

Thermenregion (2332 hectares) got its name from old public spas in the region. The climate is characterized by hot, arid summers and cold winters, and the soil is stony and sparing, with occasionally heavy loam. The main products are Neuburger and Weissburgunder (Pinot Blanc).

Traisental (682 hectares) is an area where grape seeds dating back to the Bronze Age were found. Highlights are the wine villages of Inzersdorf, Getzersdorf and Reichersdorf, where Grüner Veltliner, Weissburgunder (Pinot Blanc) and Blauburgunder (Pinot Noir) are produced. The Renaissance castle, Walpersdorf, and the museum in Inzersdorf are also key places to visit.

Wachau (1390 hectares) is the area surrounding the monastery of Melk, one of Austria's baroque masterpieces. The steep terraced vineyards complement the idyllic villages, castle ruins and orchards that line the banks of the Danube River. Grüner Veltliner and Riesling are the main products.

Weinviertel (15,892 hectares) is Austria's most extensive sub-region and a wonderful place for culinary or wine touring. Bicycle and walking paths lead visitors through charming villages and impressive castles. In western Weinviertel is the 700-year-old town of Retz, with an underground network of wine cellars that is over 26 kilometers long.

II. Burgenland

This wine region encompasses over 20,000 hectares and accounts for 36% of the Austria's wine production.

Mittelburgenland (1877 hectares) is also nicknamed "Blaufränkisch Land," as that wine is the main product of the region. This hilly, wooded region is home to the wine villages of Horitschon, Deutschkreuz, Neckenmarkt and Lutzmannsburg.

Neusiedlersee (8326 hectares) has a distinctly flat landscape and the area around Lake Neusiedl is almost completely covered with grapevines. The earth with its loess, black soil, gravel and sand produce mainly Welschriesling and Weissburgunder.

Neusiedlersee-Hügelland (3911 hectares) is a region filled with many charming villages, including Rust, a town famous for the "elixir" that winemakers provided for Emperor Leopold and his troops as they fought off the Turks and Hungarians in the seventeenth century. Rust is also home to the sweet Ausbruch wines and to Austria's Wine Academy, the first German-speaking institution of its kind in the country.

Südburgenland (448 hectares) produces mainly Blaufränkisch, Zweigelt and Welschriesling. The wine museum in Moschendorf covers the region's history.

III. Styria (Steiermark)

This region consists of over 2800 hectares and accounts for 5% of the country's wine production.

Südoststeiermark (1115 hectares) is home to nearly 2,200 growers, making the average vineyard size only half a hectare. Volcanic and basalt soils, along with sandy loam, help produce Welschriesling, Weissburgunder, and the Traminer from the area of Klöch.

Südsteiermark (1741 hectares) is a region that is often referred to as "Austria's Tuscany" because of the rows and rows of vines that line the steep slopes of its hills. The soil is rich in slate, sand, marl and limestone, producing Welschriesling, Sauvignon Blanc and Chardonnay (Morillon).

Weststeiermark (432 hectares) is home of the famous Austrian Schilcher, a rosé made from lightly pressed Blauer Wildbacher grapes. The Schilcher is a dry, fruity, salmon-colored wine with herbal overtones. According to Austrian law, Blauer Wildbacher can only be grown in the Steiermark region.

IV. Vienna (Wien)

The wine-growing region around Vienna consists of over 700 hectares and accounts for 1% of the country's wine production. Slate, gravel and loess soils lead to the production of Grüner Veltliner, Neuburger, Traminer, Weissburgunder, Chardonnay and Riesling. Vienna is the only capital in the world that has commercial vineyards within its city limits. It is believed that a wine-growing culture already existed here when the city was the Celtic village of Vedunia and the Roman military port of Vindobona, but the oldest Viennese vineyards are documented around 1132. Today the city is dominated by a "Heurige," or "wine inn," culture, where local winemakers sell their own wines and foods in inns or bars. There are about 180 licensed Heurige and almost 500 winemakers in Vienna.

RESOURCES FOR TRAVELERS

The following sources provide information for travelers regarding Culinary, Wine and Brewery tours of Austria:

The Austrian National Tourist Office (for North American residents)
Travel Information Center
P.O. Box 1142
New York, NY 10108-1142
Phone (212) 944-6880
www.anto.com

Austrian Wine Marketing Board
(Osterreichische Weinmarketing Servicegesellschaft)
Gumpendorfer Strabe 5
1060 Vienna
Austria

The Austrian Wine Academy
(Weinakademie Osterreich)
Haupstraße 81
7071 Rust
Austria
Phone (+43) 2685-453
Fax (+43) 2685-6431

Index

220

Inhaltsverzeichnis

225

Cookbooks of interest from Hippocrene . . .

All Along the Danube, Expanded Edition

Recipes from Germany, Austria, Czechoslovakia, Yugoslavia, Hungary, Romania, and Bulgaria

Marina Polvay

Now updated with a section on classic Central European wines!

For novices and gourmets, this unique cookbook offers a tempting variety of over 300 Central European recipes from the shores of the Danube River, bringing Old World flavor to today's dishes.

357 pages • 5½ x 8½ • numerous b/w photos & illustrations • 0-7818-0806-5 • $14.95pb • (479)

All Along the Rhine

Recipes, Wines and Lore from Germany, France, Switzerland, Austria, Liechtenstein and Holland

Kay Shaw Nelson

This wonderful collection of over 130 Rhine recipes spans the range of home cooking, from Appetizers, Soups, Main Courses, and Side Dishes, to Desserts and Beverages. Among the recipes included are "Cheese Fondue," "Balzers Split Pea-Sausage Stew," "Alpine Sauerkraut Soup," "Bratwurst in Beer," and "Pears in Red Wine." Each chapter covers the culinary history and winemaking tradition of a different Rhine region. The literary excerpts, legends and lore throughout the book will enchant the reader-chef on this journey down one of the world's most famous rivers.

230 pages • b/w photos • 5½ x 8½ • 0-7818-0830-8 • $24.95 hc • (89)

Taste of Romania, Expanded Edition

Nicolae Klepper

Now updated with a chapter of Romanian-Jewish Recipes!

"A brilliant cultural and culinary history . . . a collection of recipes to be treasured, tested and enjoyed."
—George Lang, owner of Café des Artistes

" . . . dishes like creamy cauliflower soup, sour cream-enriched *mamaliga* (the Romanian polenta), lamb stewed in sauerkraut juice and scallions, and *mititei* (exactly like the ones I tasted so long ago in Bucharest) are simple and appealing . . . Klepper paints a pretty picture of his native country's culinary possibilities."
—Colman Andrews, *Saveur* magazine

A real taste of both Old World and modern Romanian culture. More than 140 recipes, including the specialty dishes of Romania's top chefs, are intermingled with fables, poetry, photos and illustrations in this comprehensive and well-organized guide to Romanian cuisine.

335 pages • 6 x 9 • photos/illustrations • 0-7818-0766-2 • $24.95hc • (462)

Hungarian Cookbook:
Old World Recipes for New World Cooks
Yolanda Nagy Fintor

These Old World recipes were brought to America by the author's grandparents, but they have been updated to accommodate today's faster-paced lifestyle. In many cases, the author presents a New World version of the recipe, in which low-fat and more readily available ingredients are substituted without compromising flavor. Hungarian cuisine is known for generous amounts of paprika, sour cream, bacon and garlic in famous dishes like "Chicken Paprika" and "Hungarian Goulash." This collection includes these classics, and spans the range of home cooking with recipes for "Bean with Sausage Soup," "Stuffed Breast of Veal," "Hungarian Creamed Spinach," and a host of tempting desserts like "Walnut Torte," and "Dilled Cottage Cheese Cake."

This is more than just a collection of 125 enticing Hungarian recipes. Eight chapters also describe the seasonal and ceremonial holidays that Hungarian-Americans celebrate today with special foods: fall grape festivals; Christmas, New Year's and Easter; summer cookouts; weddings and baptisms. The book also includes culinary tips, a glossary of terms and explanations about the Hungarian language.

182 pages • 5 ½ x 8 ¼ • $24.95hc • 0-7818-0828-6 • (47)

Poland's Gourmet Cuisine
Bernard Lussiana and Mary Pininska
Photography by Jaroslaw Madejski

Here is Poland's cuisine as you've never seen it before! Bernard Lussiana, Executive Chef of Warsaw's celebrated Hotel Bristol, has taken traditional Polish dishes, like pierogi, golabki and flaki, and re-interpreted them in fresh, sophisticated and delicious new ways. Inspired by the beauty and spirit of the nation's lakes, rivers and plains, Lussiana takes bold new culinary initiatives with Poland's wealth of indigenous ingredients like buckwheat, poppyseeds, carp, pike, beetroot, suckling pig, wild boar, horseradish and dill, creating not only new dishes, but paving the way for a new era in Polish culinary history. Among the 52 recipes included are such exquisite offerings as "Delicate stew of perch fillet, chanterelles and ceps flavored with marjoram," "Barley consommé served with quenelles of smoked game," "Pan-fried fillet of lamb served with a juice of fresh coriander and saffron kasza," and "Iced parfait flavored with zbozowa coffee."

Along with stunning, full-color food photographs of every recipe, are captivating photographs of the beautiful Polish countryside, and fragments of some of Poland's most evocative poetry. The recipes are provided in a step-by-step format and all adapted for the North American kitchen. A mingling of the senses—visual, artistic, literary, sensual and culinary—this book unfolds to reveal a dream of Poland rarely glimpsed.

143 pages • 9¼ x 11¼ • color photographs throughout • $35.00 hc • 0-7818-0790-5 • (98)

Polish Heritage Cookery, Illustrated Edition

Robert and Maria Strybel

- Over 2,200 authentic recipes!
- Entire chapters on dumplings, potato dishes, sausage-making, babkas and more!
- American weights and measures
- Modern shortcuts and substitutes for health-conscious dining
- Each recipe indexed in English and Polish

"An encyclopedia of Polish cookery and a wonderful thing to have!"

—Julia Child, *Good Morning America*

"*Polish Heritage Cookery* is the best [Polish] cookbook printed in English on the market. It is well-organized, informative, interlaced with historical background on Polish foods and eating habits, with easy-to-follow recipes readily prepared in American kitchens and, above all, its fun to read."

—*Polish American Cultural Network*

915 pages • 6 x 9 • 16 pages color photographs • over 2,200 recipes • $39.95hc • 0-7818-0558-9 • (658)

Bavarian Cooking

Olli Leeb

With over 300 recipes, this lovely collector's item cookbook covers every aspect of Bavarian cuisine from drinks, salads and breads, to main courses and desserts. Some traditional recipes include Suckling Pig, Stuffed Pigeons, Hot Sprout Salad, Mushrooms in Cream Sauce, Toasted Potato Dumplings, and of course, the world-famous Bavarian Cream. Includes charming line drawings, nine color photos, and an illustrated map of Old Bavaria.

176 pages • 6½ x 8¼ • 0-7818-0561-9 • $25.00hc • (659)

The Best of Czech Cooking, Expanded Edition

Peter Trnka

Now expanded with 3 new chapters on Pork, Mushrooms, and Drinks, this popular Hippocrene cookbook is better than ever. Czech cuisine emphasizes delicious soups, salads, dumplings, hearty meat dishes, vegetables and desserts, with recipes that rely on the subtle flavors of fresh ingredients. This new edition includes "Vepro-knedlo-zelo," a classic dish of pork, cabbage and dumplings; an informative chapter about gathering, storing and using wild mushrooms; and a section on aperitifs, wine and beers, including the world-famous Czech Pilsner Urquell beer.

403 pages • 5½ x 8¼ • 0-7818-0805-7 • $24.95hc • (456)

The Best of Slovak Cooking

Sylvia & John Lorinc

This cookbook features over 100 easy-to-follow Slovak recipes. Along with creative preparation of certain staples such as potatoes, cabbage and noodles, Slovak cuisine is also noted for its pastries, rich butter and cream dishes, and pork specialties. Among the chapters included are: Soups, Vegetables & Side Dishes, Main Dishes, and Desserts & Breads. All recipes are adapted for the North American kitchen.

138 pages • 5½ x 8¼ • 0-7818-0765-4 • $22.50hc • (543)

Best of Albanian Cooking

Klementina and R. John Hysa

These 100 recipes cover every aspect of the Albanian meal, with sections on inviting meze-s (appetizers) and turshi-s (pickles) through Meat, Poultry and Rabbit, Vegetables, Soups, Fish, Pasta and Pies, Sauces, Compotes and Desserts, and Drinks. Also included are classic dishes like hearty tavë kosi (Baked Lamb with Yogurt), delicately seasoned Midhje në verë të bardhë (Mussels in White Wine), and Thëllëzë me ullinj (Grouse and Olives), all adapted for the North American kitchen.

168 pages • 5½ x 8½ • 0-7818-0609-7 • $22.50hc • (721)

Traditional Bulgarian Cooking

Atanas Slavov

This collection of over 125 authentic recipes, the first comprehensive Bulgarian cookbook published in English, spans the range of home cooking: including many stews and hearty soups using lamb or poultry and grilled meats, vegetable and cheese pastries; desserts of sweetmeats rich in sugar and honey, puddings, and dried fruit compotes.

200 pages • 5½ x 8½ • 0-7818-0581-3 • $22.50hc • (681)

Prices subject to change without prior notice. To order Hippocrene Books, contact your local bookstore, visit www.hippocrenebooks.com, call (718) 454-2366, or write to: Hippocrene Books, 171 Madison Avenue, New York, NY 10016. Please enclose check or money order adding $5.00 shipping (UPS) for the first book and $.50 for each additional title.